Praise for *The Secret His...*

"With equal parts sugar, spice, ~~~~~~~~~~~~~, Linda Raedisch takes us on a rollicking adventure through the surprising (and at times surprisingly dark!) histories behind our favorite holiday treats (and ones we'd never heard of but now can't wait to try!), then lays out easy-to-follow steps to make and decorate them. Inventive, captivating, and so very smart. I learned a *ton* from this book, which will no doubt become a staple of the Scholarly Cookbook genre (and if that's not a thing, it is now!). Truly the best kind of gift, Christmas or other."

—Wendy Mass, author of the *New York Times*
bestselling novel, *The Candymakers*

"If Mrs. Beaton, Hildegard, and The Two Fat Ladies got together with a medieval monk and had a love child, it would be *The Secret History of Christmas Baking*. Linda Raedisch has made me rethink my aversion to fruitcake. Oh, and the book's peppered with crafts for when you can't face down one more cookie. I am insanely jealous that I did not write this book."

—Natalie Zaman, award-winning author of
Magical Destinations of the Northeast and *Color and Conjure*

"Fun and engaging… A holiday gift of a book, full of fascinating history, recipes that re-create the historical Christmas of the past, and present ideas for creating new traditions… A joy to read, both enlightening and mouthwatering! You'll find yourself saying, 'I never knew that!' and wanting to try some of the traditional Christmas foods yourself."

—Jack Santino, PhD, folklorist and author of
Halloween and Other Festivals of Life and Death

"As an author and a historian, I was delighted to find that this work is much more than a cookbook. Linda Raedisch gives us a unique historical narrative and, along with each recipe, fascinating details that provide insights of how each dish is related to ... times long past."

—Robert A. Mayers, author of
Searching for Yankee Doodle

"Linda Raedisch's latest book describes itself as *The Secret History of Christmas Baking*, but it is much more than that. It is a fascinating history of the remarkably violent medieval spice trade ... For serious bakers, it describes the uses of a variety of spices, nuts, and other rare ingredients ... It provides the promised history of baking with a variety of historical recipes, some made primarily at Christmas and some not, from Europe and Asia, as well as DIY instructions for paper crafts displayed at Christmastime in one culture or another."

—Tom A. Jerman, author of *Santa Claus Worldwide*

"*The Secret History of Christmas Baking* is many things: a compendium of (sometimes strange) culinary delights, a personal remembrance of family traditions, and a whirlwind tour of the sometimes sinister, occasionally tragic, and always colorful backstories of ingredients, recipes, methods, and madnesses that flavor our most beloved holiday treats. Linda Raedisch tempers a historian's eye with wry humor and reverence. This book is a must-read for any baker, marzipan enthusiast, or kitchen witch."

—Caren Gussoff Sumption, contributing writer for
Krampusnacht: Twelve Nights of Krampus

the Secret History of Christmas baking

© Andrew Snyder

About the Author

Linda Raedisch has been contributing crafts, recipes, and ethnobotanical lore to *Llewellyn's Herbal Almanac* since 2012. Outside the kitchen, she has special interests in needlework, minority languages, and exploring the suburban jungle. You can follow her culinary, crafting, and linguistic adventures at Instagram@lindaraedisch.

from the author of
The Old Magic of Christmas

Linda Raedisch

the secret history of Christmas baking

recipes & stories
from tomb offerings to
gingerbread boys

Llewellyn Publications · Woodbury, Minnesota

FIRST EDITION
Second Printing, 2023

Cover design by Cassie Willett
Cover illustration by Nicole Raskin
Interior illustrations by the Llewellyn Art Department

Photography is used for illustrative purposes only. The persons depicted may not
endorse or represent the book's subject.

Llewellyn Publications is a registered trademark of Llewellyn Worldwide Ltd.

Library of Congress Cataloging-in-Publication Data
Names: Raedisch, Linda, author.
Title: The secret history of Christmas baking : recipes & stories from tomb
offerings to gingerbread boy / Linda Raedisch.
Description: First edition. | Woodbury, MN : Llewellyn Publications, 2023.
| Includes bibliographical references and index.
Identifiers: LCCN 2023020104 (print) | LCCN 2023020105 (ebook) | ISBN
9780738772356 | ISBN 9780738772509 (ebook)
Subjects: LCSH: Christmas cooking. | Christmas cooking—History. | Baking.
| Gingerbread. | LCGFT: Cookbooks
Classification: LCC TX739.2.C45 R34 2023 (print) | LCC TX739.2.C45
(ebook) | DDC 641.5/686—dc23/eng/20230711
LC record available at https://lccn.loc.gov/2023020104
LC ebook record available at https://lccn.loc.gov/2023020105

Llewellyn Publications
A Division of Llewellyn Worldwide Ltd.
2143 Wooddale Drive
Woodbury, MN 55125-2989
www.llewellyn.com

Printed in the United States of America

Other Books by Linda Raedisch

Lore of Old Elfland

Old Magic of Christmas

Dedication

In memory of all the planters, harvesters, processors, and artisans whose names we'll never know.

Acknowledgments

For every helpful friend, relative, or acquaintance named in this book, there were two or three more who were kind enough to sample my experiments or let me pick their brains. Shout-out to my New Providence neighbors, my coworkers at the New Providence Memorial Library, the New Providence Historical Society, and my online Plattdüütsche Familie. Special thanks also to my aunt, Erika Ernst, for introducing me to the story of St. Catherine's Church at Jellenbek.

Contents

Introduction

When the idea of writing a historical Christmas baking book first occurred to me, I thought I would make it all about gingerbread. My family is mostly German, a fact reflected in the recipes we make at Christmastime, and I was already well versed in *Lebkuchen*, gingerbread's German cousin. Because we're also American, I was eager to trace the Anglo-American gingerbread boy back to his roots in the medieval and possibly Classical worlds. I had no idea how circuitous that journey would be, or how unsettling.

There's no question that American soft gingerbread, Ashkenazi *lekach*, and German Lebkuchen are all closely related. They're all cakes, too, but when I followed the breadcrumbs back to the sticky *panforte*, a dessert that's been holding court at Italian Christmas tables since the Middle Ages, I found myself teetering on the border between cake and confection. I'm not a confectioner—using a candy thermometer feels too much like science—but the story of panforte is incomplete without mentioning torrone, a sweetmeat whose lineage pointed this hapless writer in two very different directions: to the feisty pagan Samnites, who were cooking up something like nougat in the shadow of their sacred walnut tree back in Roman times, and to the court kitchens of early medieval Baghdad, where the art of candy making began.

Torrone is all right, but in my opinion, the medieval Arab confectioners' crowning achievement was the invention of marzipan—a paste of sugar, almonds, and uncertain etymology. Marzipan can be eaten on its own, but it's also one of the key ingredients in one of the finest kinds of Lebkuchen. If I was going to tell the story of Lebkuchen, I realized, I was going to have to tell the story of marzipan, too. I also had to learn how to make it.

Nowadays, Danish marzipan is available in the baking aisle of my grocery store, but when I was growing up, the only way to get it was to go to Germany or to wait until the package my German grandmother had sent was opened on Christmas Eve. This was in the days when overseas packages came wrapped in smooth brown paper and tied up with string. The package wasn't particularly large, but the foreign postage stamps and the thinness of that brown paper made it look like something from another world when it appeared under the Christmas tree in late December. My sister and I regarded the chocolate-covered marzipan loaves my grandmother always included as sacred food, the recipe for which was a mystery. For my mother, they were a taste of home.

Those red-foil-wrapped "black breads," as they're called, are a lot easier to get today, but making my own marzipan at home makes me feel like a magician. Is my marzipan as good as what you can buy in my mother's hometown of Lübeck, the marzipan capital of the world? Maybe not. But for stirring into an Elisenlebkuchen dough or folding inside a Stollen log, it does very well. It even makes a nice potato.

But before we start baking, let's return to the subject of gingerbread. At first glance, the crispy, molded *speculaas* cookie enjoyed by so many at Christmastime does not appear to be at all related to the soft, braided challah served with dinner on the Jewish Sabbath, but they're both part of the same story. What happens when a monotheistic, yeast-bread-baking people enters polytheistic griddle cake territory? Interesting things, that's what, foremost among them the *duivekater*, a bone-shaped pastry that may have developed as a substitute for a livelier winter sacrifice—more about that in chapter 5.

Though our ancestors came from Saxony in eastern Germany and the walled city of Lübeck in the stormy north, my family treasures our Nuremberger Lebkuchen tins, some of which are as big as breadboxes, others just the right size for keeping tea bags. Lebkuchen is the southern German city of Nuremberg's gift to the world, and the five-hundred-year-old Christkindlesmarkt where you can buy it is a dazzling vision of Christmas at its best.[1] The shining figure of the Christkind, Nuremberg's kindly, cross-dressing ambassador, was created in 1948 as a way of putting the city's darkest chapter behind it, but Nuremberg's history of antisemitism long predates the Third Reich. It should not be forgotten that the Frauenkirche, the church in which the Christkind first appears in late autumn, was built on the ashes of the medieval Jewish quarter, or that the Jewish bakers whose ancestors helped transform a tough little honey cake into the refined cookie from which the city continues to draw its fame were excluded from the guild of Lebkuchen bakers.

1. While Nuremberg is located in the province of Bavaria, the Nurembergers are not culturally Bavarians but Franks or "Franconians." They have their own traditional costumes and their own regional dialect.

I was aware when I embarked on this project that the timelines of most medieval European cities were punctuated by outbreaks of antisemitic violence, but that wasn't all I had to reckon with.

"What are you working on?" my friends would ask me when I dropped by with my culinary experiments.

"A history of Christmas baking."

"That sounds like fun."

"It's actually pretty dark."

"What's dark about Christmas baking?"

"Everything."

The baking of cookies and cakes didn't come into its own until the end of the Middle Ages when Europeans were able to secure a steady supply of sugar. When I typed "sugar" into my library's online catalog, the screen lit up with a dozen books about how we could and should learn to live without it. If only those books had been written five hundred years ago. The displacement, enslavement, and obliteration of peoples caused by the Early Modern appetite for the juice of this tropical grass was a centuries-long catastrophe, the effects of which are still felt today.

Before sugar became a food group, it was just another spice, one of many whose backstories I tell in this book. Medieval and Early Modern Europeans were passionate about their spices, but cloves, cinnamon, and nutmeg wouldn't grow on European soil. In fact, it wasn't until the end of the Middle Ages that the locations of the lands where they did grow became known to anyone other than those who harvested them and the Arab middlemen who handled their export. The harder a spice was to acquire, the more blood was shed for it—

so much so that, at one point, I started thinking of this book as "the violent history of Christmas baking."

That said, there's a lot of fun to be had in these pages—we're baking, after all!—so let's not throw the Befanas out with the bathwater.[2] There are even a few uplifting turns, between the massacres, and much that is simply mystifying, like the tendency of ancient Egyptian figures, both historical and semihistorical, to present themselves on almost every leg of the journey, often where I had least expected to find them—in the snowy Alps or at the edge of a northern forest. There are plenty of heroes, too, many of them unsung, a few tragic, some only recently snatched from the jaws of obscurity.

Some writers pride themselves on finding a pagan origin for everything from the star at the top of the Christmas tree to the stockings hanging by the fire. I did a little of that in an earlier book, *The Old Magic of Christmas*, and, judging by its success, this is a popular approach. This time, however, I'm more interested in what kinds of cookies the kids are putting out with their stockings, who was the first to bake them, and where those early bakers got their ingredients. As I did in *Old Magic*, I'll be keeping you busy both in the kitchen and at the crafting table, but this book is a lot shorter on gauzy spirits, and a lot longer on sailors, saints, and artisans—though there is no shortage of the macabre. We eat to live, but at Christmastime, we also eat to remember the dead.

Our travels will be taking us deep into the history of Christendom but also far beyond its borders, both in time and space. I hope readers of other faiths, or no faith, will come

---

2. Befanas: Italian Epiphany witches, figures as beloved as our own Santa Claus, though not as pretty.

along for the ride. Christian readers might wonder why there are so many witches in this book. The answer is, I like witches, and, like those ancient Egyptians, the witches insisted on being included.

The story of even the humblest Christmas cookie is a global story. Coming from a German baking—and eating—tradition, it was natural for me to give this book a Central European focus, but Italy has been influencing the lands now known as Germany since the days of the Etruscans, especially when it comes to food, so we'll be spending significant amounts of time in Venice, Siena, and Verona. Germany, via Victorian England, may have given America the Christmas tree, but Americans, specifically the Maya, Aztecs, and Taino, gave chocolate, vanilla, and allspice to the world. And though sugar was first cultivated in Asia, sugar production didn't reach a fever pitch until West Africans were forced to grow and process it in the Caribbean.

I live not far from New York City, which means I have personal access to a wide variety of people from a wide variety of places. If I ran into you at any time in the last three years, I probably asked you how you felt about Christmas, even if you weren't in the habit of celebrating it yourself, even if you had never baked a batch of cookies, or, as in the case of my friend Steve, weren't even sure where your oven was. Those of you who gave the most interesting answers will find yourselves in these pages. I had a lot of answers to choose from. Not everyone likes Christmas, but pretty much everyone has something to say about it, whether they're from India, Pennsylvania, or the edge of the Sonoran Desert, and Christmas foods loom large in the narratives.

You may be surprised to learn that few of the following recipes started out as Christmas fare; Christmas is simply where they have come to roost. December is the time to bring heirloom decorations down from the attic, pull yellowed recipe cards out from under the takeout menus in the kitchen drawer, and reach into the darkest shadows of the spice cabinet for the cloves, nutmeg, and ginger we haven't used all year. All recipes were new at one time, and in the Middle Ages it was the height of fashion to include heavily spiced and sugared foods in all courses of a meal, a taste that lives on in traditional Ashkenazi cooking where cinnamon cozies up to meat, carrots, cabbage, and onions.[3] In an age when you could pay your taxes in peppercorns, spicy food was also a sign of status. You may have heard that the medieval desire for spices was rooted in the need to mask the taste of rotten meat, but our ancestors were no fools. No one expected fresh meat to last through the summer; that's why slaughtering was done in the fall. Any meat that couldn't be consumed by the twelfth day of Christmas was salted or smoked.

We don't need spices. Whether or not to use them has always been a matter of preference and of cultural and religious expression. When sweet pigeon pies and cinnamon-laced rabbit stews fell out of favor, sugar retired to the end of the meal. The spices, no longer an indication of class, were then reserved for the reckless ostentation of Christmas, their brash aromas reminding us of celebrations long past and loved ones long gone. Just as we put the Christmas tree in the same spot every year and decorate it ritually with the same ornaments, a

---

3. Jonathan Katz, "Gingerbread Cake," Flavors of Diaspora, January 16, 2019, https://flavorsofdiaspora.com/category/elite-dishes/.

great-grandmother's gingerbread recipe becomes canon, the eating of it a sacrament.

In Amsterdam, when the *pepernoten* start to fly, filling the air with the scents of clove, nutmeg, and cinnamon, it means that St. Nicholas will soon be spurring his white horse over the sleet-spotted cobbles. In Dresden, bakers dancing in the streets with giant "snow brooms" (whisks) and saberlike Stollen knives herald the beginning of the Christmas baking season, while towering displays of boxed panettone in stores the world over remind us to start buying presents. In many American households, the tree goes up on Thanksgiving night, while cookie baking is put off until Christmas Eve afternoon, a reversal of the German tradition in which the baking begins at the end of November and the tree doesn't even enter the house until December 24. If you stop by my mother's house the Saturday morning after Thanksgiving, you'll find sheets of anise drops—the working mother's answer to the more time-consuming *Springerle*—drying on the dining room table. You might get to try one by the light of the first Advent candle on Sunday, but the rest will be sealed away until later in the season.

The medieval Advent, or "St. Martin's Lent," was a period of fasting. Meat, eggs, dairy, and other "luxury" foods were forbidden between St. Martin's Day (November 11) and Christmas, but "medicinal" pastries flavored with sugar, rose water, citron, orange peel, and almonds—items available only from the apothecary—were permitted. Credit for the blend of "Christmas spices" we still use today must go, at least in part, to thirteenth-century theologian Thomas Aquinas, who proclaimed that the eating of sugar and other spices did not count as breaking the Advent fast.[4] (He also endorsed bathing and a glass of wine at bedtime, so be sure to thank him for that, too.) In a population riddled by intestinal parasites, people were always hungry for a cure, and children especially were fed quantities of marzipan and gingerbread to aid their digestion, a practice that continued in the New World with recipes like "dyspepsia bread," made with wheatmeal and molasses.[5]

Sugar in all its forms, from the darkest molasses to the nearly white crystalline sugar that only royalty could afford, was treated as both a medicine and a spice when it first appeared in Europe. Even when sugar became available to the lower classes, it was doled out not by the cup but by the teaspoon by the all-powerful apothecaries. The sweet almonds that make up the bulk of a marzipan loaf are harmless, but you needed a prescription for the poisonous bitter almonds that give it its distinctive flavor. (Apothecaries used to stock powdered Egyptian mummy, too, but rest assured that none of the recipes in this book call for it.)

The apothecaries who supplied these "drugs" took their cues from the physicians of the day, medical handbooks doing much to drive the initial desire for sugar and spice. Tenth-century Christian convert and physician Constantine the African's *Salernitan Health Regimen* was a bestseller, for those who could afford a handwritten copy, as were Nostradamus's *Treatise on Cosmetics and Conserves* (1555) and Partridge's *The treasure of commodious conceites, and hidden secrets, commonly called the good huswives closet of provisions for the health of*

4. Sidney W. Mintz, *Sweetness and Power: The Place of Sugar in Modern History* (New York: Penguin Books, 1985), 98.

5. Sarah Josepha Hale, *Early American Cookery: "The Good Housekeeper," 1841* (Mineola, NY: Dover Publications, 1996), 27.

her household (1584), *conceite* being an early term for confection. With recipes for candied lemon slices, candy-shelled "comfits," and electuaries (pastes of honey, sugar, spices, and sometimes gold), many of these books read more like candy making manuals than medical treatises.

The need to cling to tradition in a world of passing fashions explains how our gingerbread became a Christmas food, but how it came to be a *Christian* food is another matter. Gingerbread, Lebkuchen, and lekach all have a common ancestor in the nut and honey cakes eaten throughout the ancient Mediterranean. Jews settled throughout the Roman Empire, from the island of Elephantine in the Nile to the far northern outpost of Cologne. They traveled widely, maintaining international networks through marriage and trade, so it's not unlikely that they were the ones responsible for turning the flat honey cakes the natives were already baking into something a little more exciting. A confectionlike cake that was eaten in Roman times (minus the chocolate), panforte, meaning "strong bread," is one of the oldest recipes in this book. Panforte is filling and travels well, making it the perfect snack for the stalwart Jewish trader to put in his pack before starting out on the long journey from Rome to Colonia (Cologne) or Augusta Vindelicorum (Bavaria's Augsburg).

Long after the fall of the Roman Empire, these traders, and the scholars who followed them, were often the only link between Christendom and the Muslim world where Classical Greek scholarship, including advice on what to eat, how, and why, was preserved in Arabic translation. The expanding Muslim empires were to have a profound effect on European cuisine, especially its confectionary. "Almond," "apricot," "lemon," "orange," "sugar," "sultana": to speak of the Christmas kitchen is to speak Arabic.

Recipes are like DNA—one finds the most permutations in the area where a dish first arose, the variety thinning out with each step away from the founding kitchen. For this reason, I have chosen recipes with deep roots. But if I were to strip every recipe down to its Dark Age essentials, I would have to cut out not just the chocolate but the sugar, making for a much tackier cookie and a much dryer cake. Bakers are innovators, trying out new ingredients as soon as they become available. If the new ingredients make their products taste better, they adopt them. Lebkuchen is still a honey cake, but for the last seven hundred years or so, it's had sugar in it, too, and many other Christmas recipes that are now touted as "ancient" include ingredients that originated in the New World.

Most of these recipes, having stood the test of time, are now icons of the Christmas season in one region or another, but they were not always so. Recipes are a form of tradition, and traditions don't stay put; they drift like snowflakes from feast to feast and faith to faith, something that can be very annoying when you're trying to gather them into easily digestible chapters. Our ancestors' Yuletide spooks now collect their offerings at the end of October, while the American candy corn has migrated from the good child's Christmas stocking to the trick-or-treater's pillowcase. The gingerbread cookies that have come to epitomize the American run-up to Christmas were once a staple of Edinburgh's Halloween fairs, and in Jewish tradition, gingerbread cake was eaten at any important occasion, as it was in the American colonies.[6]

---

6. F. Marian McNeill, *Hallowe'en: Its Origins, Rites and Ceremonies in Scottish Tradition* (Edinburgh: The Albyn Press, 1970), 57.

Honey cake still shows up at Rosh Hashanah, but for the most part, Jewish gingerbread has succumbed to one of the reactions and re-reactions that can occur between cultures. In the early twentieth century, many of New York's Jewish immigrants put up Christmas trees, as they had done at home in Austria and Germany. After the horrors of World War II, the practice largely stopped. When gingerbread reinvented itself as the quintessential American Christmas cookie, Jewish gingerbread took a step back. The idea seems to be that while the American Hannukah, a minor holiday in the Old World, can give the American Christmas a run for its money, it should not be caught merging with it, at least not publicly.[7]

Christmas and nuptial traditions, however, have successfully overlapped. Gingerbread, with its expensive spices, was served at both Jewish and early American weddings, and the mammoth, brandy-soaked plum cake with which Victoria and Albert celebrated their union in 1840 was the same kind of cake the royal family would have enjoyed at Christmas. The plum cake's cousin, the Caribbean Black Cake, appears on Christmas tables as well as at weddings, dressed up in marzipan and royal icing. Wedding receptions and Christmas dinners are occasions for bringing out one's finest: the finest clothes, the finest china, the finest ingredients to make the finest cake.

Getting Ready

It took an army to bake, soak, and frost Victoria and Albert's wedding cake. We won't be tackling anything so ambitious.

---

7. The American Thanksgiving has no such boundaries. On the rare occasion that it falls during or near Hanukkah, it is, in many households, acceptable to put cranberry sauce on the latkes.

The recipes in this book are for small batches, and they're all designed for a kitchen staff of one. Though I've been baking all my life, and I've learned from the best, I'm not a professional baker. If you keep stricter rules than the ones I've set, do follow them, and do double the recipes you like after the first try. Christmas baking is all about sharing, over coffee or tea by the light of the Advent candles and by sending your Christmas cakes, breads, and cookies out into the world. Because presentation is 90 percent, I've included crafts along the way for dressing up your parcels, tins, and cookie plates.

Almost all the recipes can be made with ingredients you'll find at the grocery store. Ideally, you'll be able to bake your pandoro in a star-shaped pan and press your speculaas into pretty wooden molds, but because few people are so well equipped, I offer substitutes and alternatives. Cookies can be stamped with found objects, and a sieve works just as well as a sifter for applying a dusting of powdered sugar. Use fresh ingredients whenever possible, but don't be afraid to make do. I prefer to grate my own nutmeg and grind aniseed with my little mortar and pestle, but if you have only powdered nutmeg and anise extract, don't let that stop you from making the recipe you want to make. (That said, if you don't have such a thing as a pepper mill, I would ask, "Why not?") A fine grater and nut grinder are good things to have, too. You can buy almond and hazelnut flour, but processing the nuts yourself is much cheaper.

Several recipes require a rolling pin. To ensure even thickness when rolling out your dough or marzipan, perch the ends of the rolling pin on two thin cutting boards or quarter-inch dowels. For molded cookies, you can press the bottom of a plastic tray mold—the kind craft stores sell for making soaps and chocolates—into your rolled-out dough. The plastic trays my frozen soup dumplings come in work nicely, too. If you're unable to lay hands on a cookie cutter, you can cut your cookies into diamonds with a knife or circles with a juice glass. You can even make crescent moons by pressing the glass into the circle a second time.

Open a cookbook from a hundred years or more ago, and you'll be staggered by the number of eggs that go into the cake recipes. Eggs, and I suppose chickens, were much smaller in the past than they are now. You don't have to go looking for eggs from heirloom chickens, but do avoid large or "jumbo" eggs, and always reach for the smallest egg in the carton. Older recipes often require you to separate the eggs, even if you'll eventually be adding the yolk to the same batter. This is because the beaten egg whites served as a leavening agent, a role that baking soda and baking powder have largely taken over.

If you're using unsalted butter, like German bakers do, add a pinch of salt. If you're using salted butter, there's no need to add more. Unless otherwise noted, always grease your baking sheet or line it with baking parchment.

One of the most important ingredients you'll need is time: time to soak the fruits for your Black Cake and the raisins for your Christstollen; time to let your dough rest or rise, either in or out of the refrigerator; time to let your Elisenlebkuchen and tiger nut cakes dry; time to let the flavors of your cookies coalesce inside their tins in the days and weeks before Christmas. You'll also need time to taste: marzipan packs an immediate, aromatic punch, panforte a peppery one, but it's only in thoughtful chewing that you'll appreciate the subtle differences between speculaas and pepernoten, Pfefferkuchen and *pierniczki.*

Many of the recipes in this book require planning, so it's good to have some of the most labor-intensive ingredients prepared ahead of time. Because you'll need candied peel, roasted and skinned hazelnuts, blanched almonds, and, oh yes, marzipan! for many if not most of the German and Italian recipes (and for the Black Cake), I've put their preparation instructions here in the introduction.

Now that you've cleared your schedule, it's time to tie your apron strings, light a candle for all those who have gone before you, and start baking! (Better scatter a little salt around, too, in case we run into any of those witches.)

Recipe

CANDIED PEEL

Ingredients

3 lemons

2 oranges (bitter oranges are what the professional bakers use, but any thick-skinned orange will do—i.e., not clementines or tangerines)

2 teaspoons salt

1 cup (200 grams) sugar

Wash the lemons and oranges. Cut each fruit in half, then in quarters. Remove the flesh. Slide the tip of the knife under the peel's inner white lining and use it to peel up as much of the white as you can. Discard the white.

Cut the peels into ¼-inch-wide strips and put them in a pot with enough water to cover them. Add a teaspoon of the salt.

Bring the water to a boil and simmer for about ten minutes. This is to remove the bitterness. Drain the peels, rinse the pot, and repeat the process with fresh water and another teaspoon of salt.

Rinse the pot again and put the peels back in along with a cup of sugar and enough water to cover. Simmer for about one hour, stirring occasionally. When the peels are soft and translucent, drain them. Spread the peels on a plate and let them dry at room temperature overnight. When they're dry, separate the lemon peels and the orange peels into two tightly sealed containers. They will keep in the refrigerator for at least a month.

Roasting and Skinning Hazelnuts

Spread your nuts in a pan or baking dish—no need to grease it; hazelnuts are oily—and bake them at 350 F (177 C) for ten minutes. Pour the hot nuts into a dish towel, tie the towel up in a bundle, and rub the nuts vigorously through the fabric. Untie the towel and remove the nuts to a plate to cool. Not all the skin will have come off, but that's okay. Grind the nuts on the finest setting of your nut grinder. They will keep in your refrigerator for a month or more.

Blanching Almonds

Put the almonds in a pot with enough water to cover and simmer them for about two minutes. Pour the water and the almonds into a bowl. Wait a few minutes. When the water has cooled enough that you can stand to reach in, take an almond out, pinch it, and watch it slip out of its skin. Careful! They have a tendency to shoot across the room. Spread the naked almonds on a dry dish towel for at least an hour before grinding them fine or storing them in the refrigerator, where they will keep for about a month.

> **Note:** Nuts keep longest with their skins on. Once the skins are off, they don't seem to keep any longer whole than they do ground—about a month in the refrigerator.

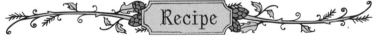

HOMEMADE MARZIPAN

Note: This marzipan won't be as fine or as stiff as the "almond candy dough" you can buy at the grocery store, but it's a lot cheaper, and its softness makes it easier to incorporate into Elisenlebkuchen and pignoli cookies, to roll out for Königsberger marzipan, and to form into a log to stick inside a Stollen. Don't worry about getting a prescription for bitter almonds; all the oil of bitter almonds you need is already in the almond extract.

Ingredients

2 cups (160 grams) blanched, ground almonds, gently patted down

1¼ cups (140 grams) powdered sugar

1½ teaspoons almond extract

1 teaspoon rose water

1 egg white (Warning: If you're going to use the marzipan to make marzipan potatoes or any other unbaked shapes, then, yes, the egg white will be consumed raw. Raw egg white may contain harmful bacteria.[8])

Makes a little more than 1 cup or 320 grams of marzipan

Put the ground almonds in a large bowl and stir in the powdered sugar. Make a well and add the almond extract, rose water, and egg white. Mix well. It will be sticky. When all ingredients are thoroughly blended, dust your hands with powdered sugar and shape the marzipan into a loaf. If you're not planning to use it right away, wrap it tightly in plastic and refrigerate. The sugar in marzipan helps it keep longer than plain ground almonds. How long? I don't know; it always gets eaten before it can go bad.

---

8. The marzipan makers are notoriously tight-lipped when it comes to their exact recipes, but Lübecker marzipan manufacturer Carstens acknowledges on their website that their products go through several heating processes. I've never seen any warning labels on any of the packages of marzipan I've bought, so either they use a binding agent other than egg white, or they heat it to eliminate any bacteria. Erasmi & Carstens GmbH, "Lübeck Marzipan," accessed January 25, 2023, https://carstens-marzipan.de/en/luebecker-marzipan/index.html.

Chapter One
The Black Land

wo things stand out from my last visit to the Penn Museum's Egyptian gallery: a blackened, three-thousand-year-old mummy toe curling out from its wrappings, and a basket of little white balls shining faintly in the light of the display case. According to the label, the balls were made of natron. I was vaguely aware that natron was used in the mummification process, but I had to do a bit of research to find out what it was: a naturally occurring combination of baking soda and soda ash that the Egyptians harvested from dry lake beds and used to make the pigment known as Egyptian blue, as well as to soak up the moisture in corpses.[9] Because natron was believed to be both spiritually and physically cleansing, baskets of natron "pellets" were presented at funerals.

Kemet was the Egyptians' own name for their country. It means "black land," and thanks to the black mud the Nile deposited on its banks each year, Kemet was a green land, too, a fertile ribbon snaking its way from Elephantine Island in the south to the alluvial fan of the Nile delta whose westernmost

---

9. "Of Mummies, Pigments, and Pretzels," McGill University for Science and Society, accessed September 21, 2022, https://www.mcgill.ca/oss/article/history -technology/mummies-pigments-and-pretzels.

city, Alexandria, would become a major player in the spice trade. Kemet was one of the first places where barley, spelt, emmer, and einkorn wheat were cultivated. Egyptian peasants had long baked plain flat cakes in the hot sand, but by the time Upper and Lower Egypt were united in the third millennium BCE, its bakers had lifted breadmaking to a high art, producing fancy loaves, twists, and artfully shaped buns not just for themselves but for the gods and the spirits of their departed loved ones. Old Kingdom bakers poured their bread batters into clay molds and baked them around a dung fire, much as the potters baked their pots. Loaves baked as offerings had to be beautiful as well as delicious, and their surfaces were pricked with pleasing, usually circular, patterns.[10]

The Nile delta was the breadbasket of the Roman Empire, Romans carrying sacks of Egyptian wheat into southern Germania along the Via Claudia.[11] I imagine the Germanic housewives were glad to get those sacks. Before that, the peoples north of the Alps had been eating a lot of cold-hardy rye and barley, grains that make for a nutritious but rather dense bread. The pharaonic bakers would no doubt have been horrified by the heavy, whole grain griddle cakes with which the northerners appeased their gods at solstice and equinox.

If Egyptian flour was the first cake flour, I wondered, could natron have been the first leavening agent? The answer is no. While the Egyptians used natron for just about everything else, there is no record of them having used it in baking. Bread and beer production went hand in hand in ancient Egypt, bakers relying on the same airborne yeasts to make their bread

---

10. Lisa Manniche, *An Ancient Egyptian Herbal* (Austin, TX: 1989), 38–41.

11. *Germania* was a Roman term designating today's modern Germany and surrounding countries, but Celts, Slavs, and Rhaetians lived there, too.

rise as the brewers did to make their beer ferment. They also used oakmoss, a kind of low-hanging lichen that had to be imported from the far shores of the Mediterranean and was probably reserved for the finest loaves, a practice the Germanic bakers never adopted.[12]

Even if a few natron pellets *had* been carried north along the Via Claudia in the early centuries CE, the natives wouldn't have needed them. The Celtic, Slavic, and Germanic peoples may not have been literate, except for a rune-master here and there, but they were chemists in their own right, and they'd already gotten the hang of making beer and tallow soap—a product their warriors treated more like hair gel than a cleaning agent. They would certainly have known how to make baking soda out of wood ashes. Later, medieval Germans would bake the sizeable antlers of the hart or red deer in lime kilns to transform the keratin into another leavening agent, *Hirschhornsalz*, "hart's horn salt," or baker's ammonia. Hirschhornsalz is still an essential ingredient in some varieties of Lebkuchen, though it is now chemically produced.

A Taste of the New Kingdom

Back in Egypt, the dead had been taking honey cakes with them to the next world for thousands of years, but the earliest evidence we have for a pastry that resembles the German Lebkuchen comes from the fifteenth-century BCE tomb of a temple official named Rekhmire. One of Rekhmire's duties was to make sure the gods in his care were properly fed; a wall painting in his tomb shows the temple bakers preparing special loaves of honey, flour, and ground tiger nuts—the dried

12. "Evernia prunastri," accessed January 28, 2023, https://scratchpad.fandom.com /wiki/Evernia_prunastri.

tubers of the grass *Cyperus esculentus,* which taste a little like hazelnuts. These tiger nut cakes were shaped into cones, not the flattened domes favored by Nuremberger Lebkuchen bakers, but the high proportion of honey and ground nuts in both cakes is similar.

In her classic book *An Ancient Egyptian Herbal,* Danish Egyptologist Lisa Manniche sketches the bare bones of the recipe Rekhmire's bakers might have followed. Manniche's proposed cakes contain only ground tiger nuts, honey, and "a little fat."[13] I have approached these cakes as a *Lebküchner* might, while using only those ingredients available to an early New Kingdom baker. The result is a sticky, nutty morsel that tastes vaguely of black tea and marzipan, neither of which it contains. I don't know what kind of oven Rekhmire's underlings had for baking the tall, conical cakes in his tomb painting, but my own oven is pretty small, which is why my cakes are smaller, too.

Recipe

REKHMIRE'S TIGER NUT CAKES

Ingredients

1 egg white

¾ cup (255 grams) honey

1 tablespoon fig preserves

¼ cup (37 grams) dates, chopped fine

1½ cups (160 grams) tiger nut flour

1 cup (142 grams) roasted, skinned, ground hazelnuts

½ teaspoon cinnamon

¼ teaspoon coriander

---

13. Manniche, *An Ancient Egyptian Herbal,* 43.

¼ teaspoon cumin
⅛ teaspoon cardamom
Pinch salt
Butter for greasing

In a medium-sized bowl, beat the egg white until stiff. Place the bowl in a larger bowl or pot half filled with hot water. Stir in honey, preserves, and dates.

Break up any lumps in the tiger nut flour before adding it to the wet mixture along with the remaining ingredients. Mix well and let sit for two hours or until moldable.

With damp hands, roll the dough into balls a teaspoonful at a time and place on a cookie sheet lined with greased baking parchment. Tiger nuts are very sticky, so this is the only time I'll ask you to both grease and paper your sheets.

Use the damp tips of your fingers to pinch each ball into a cone. Let sit for forty-eight hours or until your dry fingertip no longer sticks to the cones when you touch them.

Bake at 325 F (165 C) on bottom rack of oven for thirty-five to forty minutes or until brown. Makes about twenty-four.

Mummy Wheat

Every so often, I come across the claim that the Christmas tree was invented in ancient Egypt, but I have yet to see anything in a tomb painting that even remotely resembles one. First of all, the Egyptians would have had to send away for one from the cedar forests of Lebanon, and by the time it arrived, even a fresh cut and a kettle full of hot water couldn't have kept the needles on. And even if the ancient Egyptians *did* invent the Christmas tree, why did no one think to put one up again until the sixteenth century—and then not in Alexandria but in Strasbourg?

The New Age myth of the ancient Egyptian Christmas tree is as persistent as that of the Victorian urban legend of mummy wheat. Egyptomania, pyramidology, mummy unrolling parties: 1840s England was an exciting time and place to be alive, especially for those who had too much time on their hands. The first so-called mummy wheat was sprouted in Bohemia in the late 1830s, but it wasn't until 1848 that the craze swept England. Poets wrote of seeds, bulbs, and peas plucked from mummies' hands to be given new life in English soil, but the gentleman farmers among whom the actual seeds circulated were all under the impression that they were descended from specimens found inside an urn that arrived at the British Museum in a shipment of mummies. By the late 1800s, the British Museum had received so many letters, both from people requesting a few grains of mummy wheat and from people wanting to know more about the ancient crops they thought they were already cultivating, that the director felt compelled to make a public statement: "Ancient Egyptian wheat will not grow."[14]

So what *were* those gentleman farmers growing in their gardens? Ordinary wheat. Mummy wheat's debunkers blamed the Arab souvenir peddlers who sold pots of modern seeds to guileless British tourists, but there were plenty of domestic hucksters, too, like William Grimstone of Grimstone's Egyptian Peas, who advertised in London's newspapers. The seed scientists of the day were almost as enthusiastic about disproving the idea that millennia-old wheat could sprout as the armchair Egyptophiles were about tending their heirloom crops. At one point, even the makers of Peek Freans biscuits weighed in. Their verdict: not possible.

Still, the myth of mummy wheat has been a hard one to quash. Bible enthusiasts liked the idea that they could grow and bake bread from the very same wheat Pharoah dreamed of in the Old Testament. Pyramidologists saw the green ears as a direct link to the practitioners of the ancient mysteries, though barley, which symbolized the resurrection of the divine Mummy King Osiris, might have been more appropriate.

The truth of the matter is that pretty much all wheat is Egyptian, since neolithic Egyptian farmers were the first to cultivate it on a grand scale. (The Sumerians, who were at least as fond of beer as their contemporaries to the west, were mostly barley farmers.) So why the obsession with mummy wheat? Northern Europeans have trouble picturing their own antiquity. Whatever monuments our ancestors might have built out of wood, withes, and sod have long ago collapsed,

---

14. G. Moshenska, "Esoteric Egyptology, Seed Science and the Myth of the Mummy Wheat," 14, *Open Library of Humanities*, February 16, 2017, https://olh .openlibhums.org/article/id/4430/.

leaving only the bare bones of places like Stonehenge, Carnac, and the hulking Scandinavian gravemounds on which priests once stood to greet the sun and to wave deceased kings off on their otherworldly journeys. Now and then, the earth offers up a finely etched sun disk or little golden ship, which is promptly ensconced in a museum case, but there is no Germanic, Celtic, Baltic, or Slavic Book of the Dead, no letters exchanged between lovers, or, except for a handful of laconic runestones, memorial inscriptions.

To trace our cultural ancestry back through Rome and Greece to Egypt where the pyramids still stand is easier and, in some ways, more rewarding. As accessible as any comic book, tomb paintings show us the sophisticated Egyptians at work, at play, and at table. Hungry for a closer connection to those painstakingly drawn priests, scribes, and dancing girls, we write songs about them, dress up like them, and flock to the museum to pay our respects whenever King Tut comes to town. We look for pharaonic traces in how we think, what we believe, and what we eat. Only sometimes is there a grain of truth in it.

Is Mummy a Spice?

Yes, but it's not *quite* as disgusting as it sounds. Had you paid a visit to your friendly neighborhood apothecary several hundred years ago, you might have found yourself standing in line behind a painter's apprentice waiting to replenish his master's supply of "mummy brown." When it was your turn at the counter, the apothecary might have prescribed the same for your persistent nosebleeds. Neither you nor the painter's apprentice, nor even the apothecary, would necessarily have known the source of the dark powder in the packet you were given.

It was not the desiccated corpse itself but its hard candy coating that medieval drug dealers sought, the word *mummy* coming from Arabic *mum*, a kind of wax. The best mummies were slathered in bitumen imported from Mesopotamia where naturally occurring deposits welled up through cracks in the earth. Bitumen is basically the same thing as asphalt and is indeed an antimicrobial. Because bitumen was expensive, many embalmers used cheaper substances like beeswax or the resin from Lebanese cedar and pistachio trees.[15] By the time the medieval tomb robbers got the idea to market it as a pharmaceutical, the dark, hardened coating had penetrated the linen bandages and even the mummy's bones, so you would invariably get a little dead Egyptian with your prescription.

In 829, the Venetians removed the mummified body of their patron saint, the apostle Mark, from its tomb in Alexandria, Egypt, not to ingest it but to venerate it in their own city. In her classic book *Venice*, Jan Morris states that the holy relics, which are supposed to lie underneath the High Altar of St. Mark's Basilica, were more than likely lost in a 976 fire.[16] If his wrappings had been coated in beeswax and resin like so many other mummies, the saint must have burned very brightly indeed. Sometime after the fire, the body, real or imagined, was said to be misplaced. After a good deal of praying, and a minor earthquake, it was found inside a crumbling pillar within the basilica,[17] an episode that reminds this writer very

15. John O'Connell, *The Book of Spice: From Anise to Zedoary* (New York: Pegasus Books, 2016), 142.

16. Jan Morris, *Venice* (London: Faber and Faber, 1993), 38.

17. Morris, *Venice*, 41.

much of the posthumous adventures of the ancient Egyptian Mummy King Osiris, whose corpse resided for a time inside a pillar hewn from a giant tamarisk tree.

Osiris was cut to pieces *before* his wife Isis wrapped him in linen bandages and turned him into the world's first mummy, but for the mummies who came after him, the bitumen that was supposed to preserve the body in the afterlife became the primary motive for tearing it apart.

Chapter Two
The Cake of Life

Any homesick trader trying to make something like Egyptian tiger nut cakes north of the Alps in the early centuries CE would have run into problems, even if he'd had the help of a good-natured Germanic Hausfrau. Working together, they could have added more hazelnuts to make up for the missing tiger nut tubers and substituted dried or mashed apples for the dates and figs. They would have needed more honey, too, since apples in those days were hard and sour, but they could easily have gotten that from the pagan beekeepers living deep in the forest.

The helpful Hausfrau—we'll call her Noris for reasons I'll explain later—might have been able to supply the coriander seeds, but any other spices would have had to come from the trader's pack. Once the dough was ready, our trader would have realized that cone-shaped cakes are difficult to bake when you have no oven—when all you have, in fact, is an open hearth and, perhaps, an iron griddle. At this point, I imagine, Noris would have stepped in and patted the cones into the shallow domes that have defined the city of Nuremberg's Elisenlebkuchen ever since.

By whichever route the first "Christmas cookie" arrived in northern Europe, we know that Jewish bakers were selling

Lebkuchenlike cakes in southern Germany by the beginning of the thirteenth century.[18] Life for Nuremberg's Jews was no picnic. The Frauenkirche (Church of the Virgin), whose Gothic brick façade looks down on Nuremberg's main Christkindlesmarkt (Christ Child Market), was built on the ruins of a synagogue destroyed on December 5, 1349, during one of the infamous Black Death Massacres of that year. Blamed for a recent outbreak of bubonic plague, over five hundred Jews lost their lives in the attack. Those Jewish-owned houses that hadn't been burned to the ground were cleared to make room for the new market square. Two years later, when the city found itself strapped for cash, the Jews were invited to return, settle in a new quarter, and start paying taxes again.[19]

The Secret Spice

Nuremberg's Christian *Lebküchner* fought for two hundred years for the right to establish their own guild, but when the city finally granted them permission in 1643, Jewish bakers were not permitted to join.[20] Today, guild membership is no longer based on religion, but in order to call their product "Nuremberger Lebkuchen," bakers must meet the guild's quality standards and do their baking either in or near Nuremberg. And, of course, they must not reveal the secret recipe.

Everyone seems to agree that five spices are needed to make Nuremberger Lebkuchen: cinnamon, nutmeg, cardamom, cloves, and a "secret" fifth spice known only to the guild. Since Lebkuchen is invariably translated into English as

---

18. Katz, "Gingerbread Cake."

19. Jewish Virtual Library, "Nuremberg," accessed September 21, 2022, https://www
.jewishvirtuallibrary.org/nuremberg.

20. Juliane Kerlen-Gramsch, "Nürnberger Leckerei," *Landlust* November/Dezember
2013, 128; Katz, "Gingerbread Cake."

"gingerbread," I'm going to go out on a limb and say it's ginger. Then again, if Lebkuchen really is an ancient cake, it could be Egyptian cumin or a pinch of the coriander that gives Lebkuchen's cousin *Magenbrot* its slightly herby taste.

Could the secret spice be black pepper? The Venetian peverino cookie and the Sienese panforte both contain black pepper, while the Dutch pepernoten, German Pfefferkuchen (pepper cake), and the gingersnaplike Swedish *peperkakor* do not. Why not? Venice exerted such a strong cultural influence on southern Germany that the Venetian word "peverino" and its cognates might have come to mean any dark, spiced cookie, just as "pepper," the most popular seasoning, became a synonym for spice. It's possible that all these cookies once contained pepper, but when the price of both pepper and sugar skyrocketed after the ravages of the Black Death, the bakers had to leave pepper out for a while.

Pepper and other spices had been welcome in the Catholic Church where they were used for anointing and burned in censers during mass, but the Protestants, at the urging of Martin Luther, did away with all that.[21] In 1525, Nuremberg opted to follow Luther's teachings and become a Protestant city, at which time they may have decided to cut down on the quantity and variety of spices in their Lebkuchen, or at least to say they had.

I thought I'd wrapped up the Lebkuchen research for this book when I attended a Christkindlmarkt in Clark, New Jersey—my first since the rise of Covid-19.[22] According to the

---

21. Michael Krondl, *The Taste of Conquest: The Rise and Fall of the Three Great Cities of Spice* (New York: Ballantine Books, 2007), 154–155.

22. *Christkindlmarkt* is the most common spelling and the one used by the Deutscher Club of Clark, NJ, where I did my shopping. The spelling *Christkindlesmarkt* seems to be unique to Nuremberg.

label on the package of Bahlsen brand Choco Contessa cookies (very similar to Elisenlebkuchen) I bought, Lebkuchen derives its signature flavor from "cinnamon, cloves, mace, and orange peel." It should be noted that the Bahlsen company, whose founder hailed from the north German city of Hannover, is neither bound by nor privy to the secrets of the Nuremberger Lebkuchen Protective Association. Obviously packaged for export, the cookies inside were identified not as "Lebkuchen," but as "gingerbread," though there was no mention of ginger. The full list of ingredients included other "spices" but did not specify which ones they were. Interestingly, it listed "ground bitter apricot kernel" instead of marzipan. Also interesting to this Egyptophile were the prominently displayed hiero-glyphs on the label. According to Bahlsen lore, the cobra, loaf of bread, and earth—a line with three dots under it—spell the ancient Egyptian word *tet*, more properly pronounced *djet*, which means "everlasting." The Bahlsen company has been using the TET logo since 1904 when it started selling its but-ter cookies in airtight, waterproof packaging. There had even been plans to build an Egyptianesque "TET-city" around the factory in Hannover, but the First World War got in the way.[23]

Whatever the identity of the fifth spice, Nuremberg was well placed to become the honey cake capital of the world. As a trading city with strong ties to Venice, it had easy access to both spices and sugars, while the surrounding forest provided honey and hazelnuts. The *Oblaten*, paper-thin wafers, that go on the bottom of Elisenlebkuchen were baked by the same nuns who baked the communion wafers, but the ones they

23. The Bahlsen Family, "History," accessed November 20, 2022, https://www .thebahlsenfamily.com/int/company/about-us/history/.

supplied to the Lebküchners were unstamped and unconsecrated. The round Elisenlebkuchen was named for Elisabeth, an ailing eighteenth-century child whose father came up with the recipe to cure her. Or so the legend goes.

ELISENLEBKUCHEN

Ingredients

2 egg whites

1 cup (200 grams) sugar

¼ cup (85 grams) honey

3 tablespoons apricot jam

3 cups (336 grams) roasted, skinned, ground hazelnuts (you can also use almonds, walnuts, or a combination thereof)

⅓ cup (75 grams) marzipan, room temperature

¼ cup (42 grams) candied orange peel

¼ cup (35 grams) candied citron or lemon peel

½ cup (60 grams) flour

1 teaspoon baking powder

½ teaspoon cinnamon

½ teaspoon nutmeg

½ teaspoon ginger (cumin? coriander? pepper?)

¼ teaspoon cardamom

⅛ teaspoon cloves

50-centimeter or larger *Backoblaten*, "baking wafers" (optional)

½ cup (72 grams) blanched whole almonds

Glaze 1

½ cup powdered sugar

4 teaspoons syrup drained from candied peel or

    2½ teaspoons water and 1½ teaspoons lemon juice

Glaze 2

½ cup (85 grams) semisweet chocolate chips

In a medium bowl, beat the egg whites with the sugar until stiff peaks form. (If you can only get soft peaks, don't worry about it.) Place the bowl in a larger bowl half filled with hot water. Stir in honey and jam, making sure none of the water in the larger bowl sloshes in. (The purpose of the water bath is to keep the honey soft so it's easier to stir in.) Remove the bowl from the hot water and stir in the ground nuts, marzipan, and peels.

In a separate bowl, mix the flour, baking powder, and spices. Stir this mixture into the wet mixture. It will be sticky. Let sit uncovered for at least one hour.

When the dough is dry enough, form it into balls a tablespoonful at a time. Keep your hands damp to keep the dough from sticking to them. Place the Backoblaten in rows on a cookie sheet and press a ball onto each. You can also press them directly onto baking parchment. Press an almond into the tops of half your Lebkuchen. (The others will be glazed with chocolate.)

Let your Lebkuchen sit for twenty-four hours.

The next day, bake them at 350 F (177 C) for twenty minutes or until they're slightly golden on top.

Prepare your lemon glaze while the first batch (with the almonds) is in the oven so you can spoon it over them as soon as they come out.

When the Lebkuchen without the almonds come out, place a few chocolate chips on each. They will melt quickly. Spread the chocolate around with the bottom of a spoon to cover evenly.

Let your Lebkuchen cool completely before storing them in an airtight container. You will need to chill the chocolate ones in the refrigerator for a while so the chocolate can set.

Rocky Mountain Harpy

The Nuremberger harpy is a friend of mine. At least, I thought she was. She greets me every morning, wings spread, from the lid of the old Nuremberger Lebkuchen tin in which I keep my tea bags. The city of Nuremberg has two official coats of arms: a small one with half a black "imperial eagle" on the left and barber pole stripes on the right, and a large one displaying a creature with a golden eagle's body and a crowned human head. The earliest example of the large coat of arms comes from a wax seal of 1200 in which the smiling creature wears a fleur-de-lis crown atop its shoulder-length curls. Is it a harpy or a very pretty king with an eagle's body? It's hard to say, but in the 1400s, the creature in question started looking a lot more feminine, and by 1700, she was wearing her hair in two tidy cinnamon rolls, her feathers creeping south to reveal a rather startling pair of breasts.

There are a number of theories why the Imperial City of Nuremberg should be represented by this *Jungfrauenalder*, "virgin eagle." It could be because the city was ruled by the constellation Virgo or because Nuremberger men were ruled by their women.[24] The idea that the virgin eagle represents the mountain nymph Noris, and that it was Noris who gave the city its name, is an appealing one, but Noris was dreamed up by seventeenth-century poets; the name Nuremberg (German, Nürnberg) more likely means "rocky mountain."

For whatever reason, our harpy's golden feathers crept back up during the 1920s, and by 1936, the creature had acquired an Adam's apple and a much squarer jaw. Officially, the modern head is described only as a "royal head," not as a "king's head."

The young eagle person on the lid of my tin is too tiny for me to discern their gender identity, but they seem to have more in common with the post-1920s coat of arms than with the fifteenth-century seal. When I turned the tin over to see which of Nuremberg's sanctioned Lebkuchen companies had commissioned it (Gebr. Seim GmbH & Co), it occurred to me to check the list of ingredients to see if the secret fifth spice had been revealed. Alas, the label said only "spices." I'm sure the little bird person knows what it is, but they're not talking.

---

24. Stephanie Heyl, "Stadt Nürnberg," accessed September 21, 2022, https://www .hdbg.eu/gemeinden/index.php/detail?rschl=9564000.

Christkind and *Rauschgoldengel*

All but destroyed during World War II, Nuremberg's Frauen-kirche was rebuilt in the 1950s and 60s, and its gallery now serves as the stage on which yet another winged creature, the Nuremberger *Christkind*, makes their first appearance of the season. Like most peripatetic Christ Children, this one is played by a teenage girl. Since 1948, it has been the Christ-kind's job to open Nuremberg's Christmas market on the Friday before the first Advent Sunday. With golden crown and golden ringlets, the Christkind looks a lot like the device on Nuremberg's coat of arms, at least from the neck up. From the neck down, this twentieth-century ambassador of Christmas wears a star-spangled robe and pleated golden wings.

Nuremberg's *Christkindlesmarkt* was named for the Christkind, but it wouldn't be complete without the huge golden angel suspended above the market's entrance or her tiny golden doppelgangers hanging amid the tinsel, lights, and Lebkuchen hearts in the market's stalls. Nuremberg was once a center of metalwork, its smiths turning out everything from golden dishes for the Holy Roman Emperors' tables to silver tinsel to hang on early Christmas trees. When the first *Rauschgoldengel*, "gold foil angels," (though they were actually made of brass foil) were made in the early 1700s, they were proba-bly meant to represent the Christ Child, who by that time had taken over many of St. Nicholas's gift-giving duties.[25] The idea that the first Rauschgoldengel was made by a grieving wood-carver in the likeness of his dead daughter was fabricated in

25. Karen Lodder, "What is a Rauschgoldengel? The legend of the Golden Angel," German Girl in America. December 6, 2018, https://germangirlinamerica.com /what-is-a-rauschgoldengel/.

the 1930s, and in fact, the earliest-known specimens had porcelain heads, not wooden.[26]

Today's Christkind's flowing garments recall Gothic church figures, but the Rauschgoldengel's tapered bodice and sharply pleated skirts were inspired by the Franconian folk costumes that crystallized during the Baroque period. And while the Christkind's hair flows over the shoulders of their robe, the Rauschgoldengel keeps hers tucked up under her crown.[27] The *rausch* in *Rauschgold* means "to murmur or rush," as in a rushing brook, which is the sound the brass foil makes when you shake it.

Craft

PAPER ANGEL

Tools and materials

1 cupcake wrapper

Gold paint

Paintbrush

Christmas wrapping paper—dull, not shiny (glue won't stick to shiny paper)

½-inch wooden bead

1 flat toothpick

Short length of gold or silver cord tied in a loop

Scissors

Glue

26. "Knisternde Himmelsboten," *Bayerische Staatszeitung*, December 19, 2016, https://www.bayerische-staatszeitung.de/staatszeitung/kultur/detailansicht-kultur/artikel/knisternde-himmelsboten.html#topPosition.

27. The blond wig is a nonoptional part of the Christkind's costume, but one does not need to be blond to play the Christkind or either of their Rauschgoldengel attendants. The only physical requirement is height: in order to be properly seen from the gallery, the Christkind must be taller than 5'2".

Fold the cupcake wrapper in quarters. Unfold it and paint it gold on one side. Let it dry.

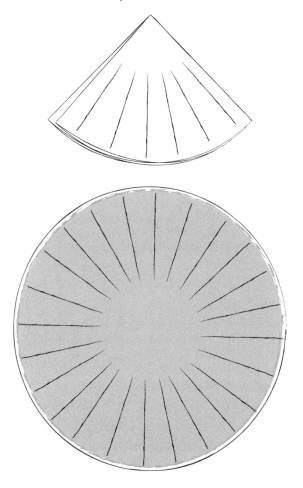

Trace the wing stencil (Figure 2a) on your wrapping paper, cut it out, and paint the plain side gold. Stencils can be found in the appendix on page 257.

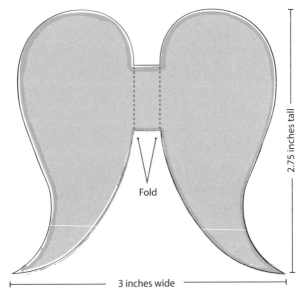

Figure 2a: Wing Stencil

Let dry. If your paper is curled, press it under a book while you work on the rest of the angel.

Use the stencils to cut the bib (Figure 2b) and three fringed pieces (Figure 2c) from your wrapping paper. Leave the bib as is, but paint the plain sides of the fringed pieces gold before you cut the fringes. These pieces will be the angel's "sleeves" and crown.

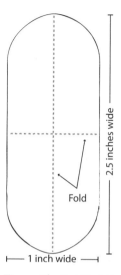

Figure 2b: Cut the bib

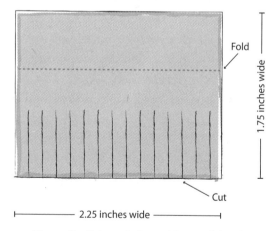

Figure 2c: Fringed pieces (three of them)

Fold the bib in quarters and cut off the corner as shown (Figure 2d). Fold the "sleeves" and crown along the dotted line in Figure 2c (on previous page).[28]

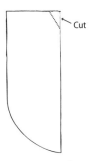

Cut

Figure 2d

Wrap a narrow strip of paper around the flat end of the toothpick so it will fit snugly inside the wooden bead. Dab the wrapped end with glue and insert it in the bead. This is your angel's head. Wrap the crown piece around her head and glue the end (Figure 2e).

Figure 2e

28. The Nuremberger Rauschgoldengel, famously, has no arms.

Insert the pointed end of the toothpick through the hole you cut in the bib (Figure 2f).

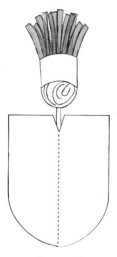

Figure 2f

Fold the cupcake wrapper in quarters and cut off the very tip of the folded point (Figure 2g).

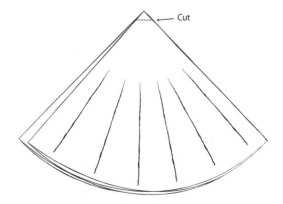

Figure 2g

These are the angel's skirts. Slide them onto the toothpick and up under the bib, about ⅛ inch. Secure with glue (Figure 2h).

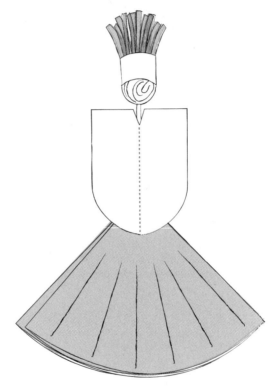

Figure 2h

Glue the sleeves to the bib so they meet at the waist. (See Figure 2i for how to position them.)

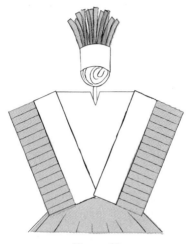

Figure 2i

Glue the loop to the angel's back (Figure 2j).

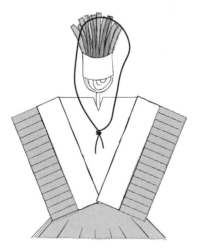

Figure 2j

Glue the wings over the loop with the golden side to the front. Paint a small square of your wrapping paper gold on one side and cut it into four narrow strips. Glue them onto bib as shown to make a star (Figure 2k).

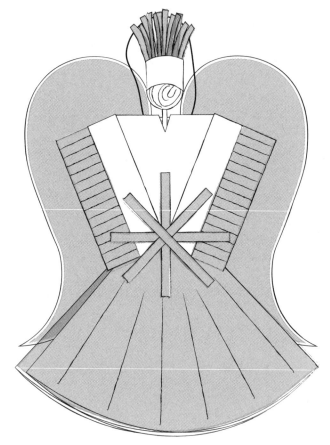

Figure 2k

Hang your angel on the tree or tie her to the ribbon on a plate of Elisenlebkuchen before you give it away.

HOMESTYLE LEBKUCHEN

For those who have neither the time nor the energy to make one of the more complicated recipes, here's one for a pan Lebkuchen that you can make quickly and easily. For years, I thought this was an old family recipe, but my mother recently told me that it came from an American neighbor. Where the neighbor got it, I have no idea. My mother has substituted black tea or coffee for the water in the original recipe, which is in keeping with some versions of the Ashkenazi lekach. My mother had never heard of lekach; she just wanted a darker color.

My mother is of the school that believes ginger does not belong in Lebkuchen. "So what do you think the secret spice is?" I asked her. "Allspice," she said. Because the New World allspice would have been a latecomer to the recipe, and because the Nuremberger bakers were bound by tradition, I disagree, but it certainly tastes good in this recipe.

Ingredients

3 eggs

2 cups (426 grams) light brown sugar

Zest of one lemon

½ cup (170 grams) honey

½ teaspoon baking soda dissolved in ¼ cup warm, strong
    black tea

3 cups (360 grams) flour

½ teaspoon cloves

1 teaspoon allspice

1 teaspoon cinnamon

1 cup (84 grams) ground almonds or hazelnuts

Glaze

1 cup (113 grams) powdered sugar
4 teaspoons milk
1 teaspoon vanilla extract

Beat sugar and eggs together. Add the remaining ingredients to make a thick dough. If too stiff, add a little more tea. Spread dough in greased jelly roll pan or large brownie pan and bake at 350 F (177 C) for twenty-five to thirty minutes until firm and golden on top.

An Egyptian in the Alps

I've mentioned the possibility of Jewish traders bringing the first spice cake recipes into Germania, but it might also have been a homesick Egyptian legionnaire. The Alpine town of St. Moritz in Switzerland is the site of the martyrdom of St. Maurice (German Moritz), a Roman military commander who, if his story can be believed, was born in Upper Egypt (i.e., southern Egypt) in 250 CE. Maurice was a Christian, something that was no longer illegal in the Roman Empire but wasn't encouraged, either. An accomplished soldier, the young Maurice was soon put in command of his own Christian Theban Legion and dispatched to Agaunum to put down a revolt in the Roman province of Gaul (France).

The plan was for Maurice and his legion to enter Gaul via the Great St. Bernard Pass (which wasn't called that yet) and start slaughtering the Celtic Gaulois as quickly as he could. When he realized that some of the Gaulois were Christians, he refused. Emperor Maximian pitched a fit, had every tenth man in Maurice's legion executed, and ordered Maurice to get on with it. When Maurice refused again, Maximian had him and the rest of his legionnaires beheaded.

A hundred years would pass before any written mention of the saint's tomb in remote Agaunum (now St. Moritz), but the story eventually picked up speed, and on Christmas Eve 961, St. Maurice was translated to Magdeburg Cathedral where his relics joined those of his fellow Egyptian, St. Catherine of Alexandria.

Stomach Bread

Magenbrot (stomach bread) is usually classified as a kind of Lebkuchen, even though it contains neither honey nor nuts. According to culinary legend, the recipe came about as a way of passing off stale bread as the more expensive Lebkuchen. In Germany, the dough is usually cut into diamonds, but in Switzerland, Magenbrot is baked in a loaf and sliced as soon as it comes out of the oven, like some varieties of Pulsnitzer Pfefferkuchen. Magenbrot is a staple of German Christmas markets, but in Switzerland, it appears at summer and autumn fairs where it's glazed in chocolate and sold in pink paper bags.

Also called *Alpenkräuterbrot*, "Alpine herb bread," or, in French, *pain d'estomac* or *pain gastrique* (which means the same as Magenbrot), it was supposed to aid digestion.

Recipe

MAGENBROT

Ingredients
1 cup (226 grams) butter, softened
1¼ cups (247 grams) sugar
2 eggs

3½ cups (390 grams) flour
1 tablespoon unsweetened cocoa powder
1 teaspoon baking powder
½ teaspoon ground aniseed
½ teaspoon cinnamon
½ teaspoon ginger
½ teaspoon coriander
¼ teaspoon cardamom
⅛ teaspoon cloves

For the Glaze
1 cup (113 grams) powdered sugar
2½ tablespoons lemon juice

Cream butter and sugar together. Beat in eggs.

Mix dry ingredients together and add a little at a time to butter/egg mixture. Turn dough onto table and knead in the remaining flour mixture until you can form a ball.

Divide the ball into four parts. Shape each part into a log and bake on two parchment-lined cookie sheets at 350 F (177 C) for thirty to thirty-five minutes or until golden.

As soon as they come out of the oven, brush loaves with the lemon glaze and cut diagonally into one-inch slices. Let cool.

Store slices separately in tightly sealed containers. Makes about fifty-six.

Chapter Three

Pepper Cake (Hold the Pepper)

he term *Lebkuchen* (life cake) can refer to the specific varieties of Lebkuchen baked in and around Nuremberg or as a generic name for all varieties of Lebkuchen, including Pfefferkuchen (pepper cake), even though Pfefferkuchen, as a rule, contains rye flour (and no pepper), and Lebkuchen (which might not have any pepper in it, either), as a rule, does not.[29] Both terms are translated as "gingerbread" in English, even though Nuremberger Lebkuchen *officially* contains no ginger.

The bear's foot on the coat of arms of the city of Pulsnitz in eastern Germany might lead you to believe that this is the place where the bear claw was invented, but Pulsnitz's specialty is Pfefferkuchen. Pulsnitzer Pfefferkuchen comes in a variety of shapes and sizes, some filled and/or glazed, others not. The white-iced *Pfeffernüsse* (pepper nuts) that you can sometimes find in American grocery stores at Christmastime are a variety of Pfefferkuchen—and don't have any pepper in them, either.

29. Sönke Krüger, "Gingerbread drama: The culinary heritage of the Germans is threatened," Welt, December 7, 2018, https://www.welt.de/iconist /essen-und-trinken/article185097354/Pfefferkuchendrama-Das-kulinarische -Erbe-der-Deutschen-ist-bedroht.html.

In Pulsnitz, it's not just the recipe that's closely guarded but also the dough, which is aged in wooden barrels for at least a few weeks before it's shaped and baked. When you inherit a Pulsnitzer bakery, you inherit the starter dough, too. (I let my Pfefferkuchen dough rest in a quiet corner of the kitchen for three days before baking.)

Are rye flour and aging the only differences between Lebkuchen and Pfefferkuchen? Well, no. There seems to be a wider variety of spices in Pfefferkuchen than in Nuremberger Lebkuchen. Also, the shapes vary, though hearts seem to be universal. But perhaps the most interesting differences are the stories that come with the cookies.

Hecate Cakes

Pfefferkuchen isn't baked only in Pulsnitz. It isn't baked only in Germany, either. The medieval city of Thorn is now Toruń, Poland, the German name living on only in the *Thorner Kathrinchen*, "little Catherines," a kind of Pfefferkuchen that originated there. In parts of Germany and Poland, St. Catherine's Day marks the beginning of the Christmas baking season, with Kathrinchen (Polish *katarzynki*) first up.

It's doubtful that St. Catherine of Alexandria ever existed, but what the girl lacks in historicity, she makes up for in the kitchen. In England, where she was often conflated with Henry VIII's ex-wife Catherine of Aragon, her feast day of November 25 was an occasion to bake "cattern cakes," cookies made with spices and dried fruit, and for children to go "cattering," an activity not unlike trick-or-treating.

Recipes for Thorner Kathrinchen vary, some indistinguishable from Pfefferkuchen, others more like the Polish pierniczki we'll be making in chapter 4. In the early thirteenth century, in the spirit of northern crusading, the militant Teutonic Order of Knights established a headquarters at Thorn as a home base for subduing the pagan Prussians, naming their fortress after a crusader castle the order had briefly possessed in the mountains of Lebanon. The Teutonic knights were followed by German merchants from Lübeck who were eager to get their hands on the honey produced by the highly efficient Prussian beekeepers. Where there is honey, there will be bakers, and by 1300, the Thorner Pfefferkuchen industry was well established. Thorn's Benedictine nuns are credited with turning out the first Kathrinchen, which they distributed among the poor on the saint's feast day.[30]

Catherine, if indeed she lived, was only eighteen when the Roman emperor Maxentius condemned her to be beaten to death on a spoked wheel. When Catherine touched the wheel, it shattered, so Maxentius had her beheaded instead. According to her legend, Catherine was a princess, though of what isn't clear. Was she a Copt, a native Egyptian Christian, or was she a member of Alexandria's Graeco-Roman ruling class? Her Greek name is usually translated as "pure," but this meaning comes from a later spelling; in earlier texts, she is Hekaterine, as in Hecate, the Greek goddess of witchcraft and sometimes the moon.

Catherine certainly had a bewitching personality: even while imprisoned, she managed to convert anyone who came within spitting distance to the strange new cult of Christianity, including Emperor Maxentius's wife, Valeria Maximilla. After having Valeria Maximilla and a host of Catherine's other converts

---

30. Bukechi, "Thorner Kathrinchen—Seit Jahrhunderten gebacken," December 26, 2021, https://bukechi.com/thorner-kathrinchen/.

burned at the stake, Maxentius proposed marriage to the young virgin, but Catherine refused. Hence the wheel.

The Kathrinchen's signature shape is not a wheel but a sort of rectangular cloud with six lobes. What it represents is a mystery even to the historians at Toruń's Living Gingerbread Museum.[31] Perhaps it is the cloud upon which the angels bore St. Catherine's body to the foot of Mt. Sinai. The Thorner Kathrinchen recipe is, of course, proprietary to the bakers of Toruń, but if you follow this recipe for Pfefferkuchen, I think you'll be pretty close. To make traditionally shaped Kathrinchen, you can order a Kathrinchen *Ausstechform*, "cookie cutter," online, but you could also make stars in honor of astronomer Nicholas Copernicus, who was born in Thorn in 1473, or crescent moons as a tribute to the Kathrinchen's namesake's namesake, Hecate.

Recipe

PFEFFERKUCHEN

Ingredients

½ cup (170 grams) honey

⅓ cup (113 grams) molasses

4 tablespoons (56 grams) butter

⅔ cup (132 grams) sugar

1 egg

1 teaspoon orange zest

1 teaspoon almond extract

1 tablespoon water

31. Muzeum Piernika, "History," accessed May 15, 2022, https://muzeumpiernika.pl/en/.

2¼ cups (270 grams) flour
½ cup (60 grams) rye flour
4 teaspoons baking powder
½ cup (42 grams) ground almonds
1 teaspoon cinnamon
½ teaspoon ginger
½ teaspoon aniseed
¼ teaspoon cardamom
¼ teaspoon coriander
⅛ teaspoon mace
⅛ teaspoon cloves
⅛ teaspoon allspice
Milk for glazing

Melt the honey and molasses together until runny. Let cool a bit.

Cream the butter and sugar. Beat in the egg. Add the orange peel and almond extract.

In another bowl, mix the flours with the other dry ingredients.

Add the cooled honey and molasses to the butter mixture, stir, and add the flour mixture a little at a time. The dough will be sticky. Shape the dough into a ball, put it in a greased bowl, and cover the top with plastic wrap or a waxed cloth. Let it sit at room temperature at least overnight.

When ready, roll the dough out to ½-inch thickness on a floured surface and cut it into shapes. You can also impress your shapes with designs (see Getting Ready in introduction). Place the cookies carefully on the cookie sheet and brush them with milk. Bake your Pfefferkuchen at 350 F (177 C) for seventeen to twenty minutes or until they're firm. Cool them completely before storing in an airtight container. Makes about forty cookies.

Variation 1

To make *Pflastersteine*, or "cobblestones," add ½ cup (80 grams) Zante currants to your dough and proceed as above. Cut the rolled-out dough into 1-inch squares. After you've brushed them with milk, sprinkle them with *Hagelzucker*, "hail sugar," to make it look like a dry snow has fallen on your cobbles. Bake as above.

To make your own Hagelzucker, mix ¼ cup (50 grams) white sugar with ½ tablespoon water. Heat both on very low heat until the sugar starts to hiss. Turn off the heat immediately and let cool. When the sugar is dry enough that you can scrape it off the bottom of the pot, do so and turn it onto a plate, being careful not to break up the little clumps that formed when you scraped it up. Let the lumps dry for at least an hour. Break up any large clumps into smaller ones and store in an airtight container until ready to use.

Variation 2

To make filled hearts, cut your dough into heart shapes. Put half on a baking sheet and use a teaspoon to place a small dollop of apple jelly in the center of each one. Run a wet fingertip around the edge of each heart and lay a plain heart on top, gently pressing the edges together. Your hearts will need to bake a little longer than ordinary Pfefferkuchen. Cover them with melted semisweet chocolate when they come out of the oven.

The Far North

Cologne, Latin *Colonia*, in Germany's Rhineland, marked the northernmost outpost of the Roman Empire on the mainland. It was in Cologne's Jewish community, well documented by 321 CE, that Yiddish was first spoken, the local dialect of Old High German enfolding everyday Aramaic as Jewish men, for a few generations at least, took Germanic wives.[32] Somehow, in between pogroms, incidents of arson, forced baptisms, and wholesale banishment, Cologne's medieval Jewish families found time to sit down and enjoy challah, the yeast-raised Sabbath Day bread, and lekach, another possible precursor of Lebkuchen. One early variety of lekach consisted of stale bread mashed with honey—an attempt, perhaps, to re-create the Italian panforte in a land where lemon peel, orange peel, and almonds were not yet readily available.

Wherever they settled, Jews were usually confined to their own quarter, but they didn't live in a vacuum. Europe's oldest Jewish communities are along trade routes in cities like

---

32. Jewish Virtual Library, "Virtual Jewish World: Cologne, Germany," accessed September 21, 2022, https://www.jewishvirtuallibrary.org /cologne-germany-virtual-jewish-history-tour.

Venice, Nuremberg, and distant Cologne. Thanks to a high literacy rate and a common written language, merchants and scholars in Spain, Italy, and Germany were able to exchange books, ritual supplies, spiritual ideas, and ingredients with their coreligionists in places as far away as Egypt, Persia, and India. Because Jewish bakers were not permitted to join or establish their own guilds, most of their culinary traditions stayed inside the community. The name *lekach* doesn't appear in writing until 1200, but Ashkenazi Jews were already baking a honeyed challah in 1105.[33] Lekach remained a loaf or round cake, but challah was at one time baked in a variety of shapes and may have influenced some of the northern Christmas breads and buns we'll be baking in later chapters.

Cologne is better known for its Carnival traditions than for Christmas, but the nearby city of Aachen is home to yet another kind of Pfefferkuchen, the *Aachener Printen*. The name *Printen* tells us that these cakes were originally "printed," or pressed into fancy wooden molds, like speculaas. There are almost as many stories about how Aachener Printen came to be as there are species of Pfefferkuchen.

The art of the molded cookie may have been introduced to the Holy Roman Empire by brass workers from the Belgian town of Dinant. The Dinanters specialized in censers, candlesticks, and other church paraphernalia as well as yellow brass cauldrons, known as *dinanderies*, that were sold at market fairs all over northern Europe.[34] The polished brass luster hanging

33. Laura Gottlieb, "The History of Honey Cake," The Nosher, September 1, 2020, https://www.myjewishlearning.com/the-nosher/the-history-of-honey-cake/.

34. Britannica, "dinanderie," accessed September 21, 2022, https://www.britannica.com/art/dinanderie.

over the heads of the "happy" couple in van Eyck's "The Arnolfini Wedding" (1434) was made by a Dinant craftsman.

In 1466, when Dinant was destroyed in a conflict known as the Liège Wars, the brass workers fled to nearby cities where, thanks to their skill set, they were welcomed. Many settled in Aachen, whose ready supply of charcoal and waterpower from the river Wurm made it perfect for setting up a foundry. Since they were already familiar with religious themes, they may have started carving Christmas cookie molds as a sideline to raise capital in their new home. For the next few hundred years, the cookies pressed into those molds would have been no different from the kind of spiced honey cookie that was ancestral to speculaas. Over time, local honey was replaced by cheaper American wildflower honey and white Caribbean sugar, most of which they acquired from the English.

When Napoleon took over the area, he blocked all trade with England. Rather than close up shop, Aachen's Printen bakers swapped in sugar beet syrup and brown rock sugar for honey and cane sugar. While brown sugar or "cassonade" is processed from sugarcane, brown rock sugar is extracted from sugar beets. Beet root syrup, *Zuckerrüben Sirup*, did not exist until about 1800 and was first produced in Silesia, at the behest of the King of Prussia, far to the east of Aachen. Happily, the lower Rhine and Cologne-Aachen Basin are particularly well suited to the cultivation of sugar beets, and the crop took off.[35] The Aachener bakers never looked back, and to this day, Aachener Printen are still made with sugar beet syrup and brown rock sugar. Because brown rock sugar is, as the name

---

35. Christine Metzger, ed,. *Culinaria Germany* (Cologne: Könemann Verlag, 1999), 234–235.

suggests, a lot more gravelly than white sugar, the dough isn't easily molded, which is why classic Printen are now baked as plain rectangles.

But that's only half the story of Aachener Printen, also called *Kräuterprinten* for the long list of spices in them. In the Middle Ages, pilgrims flocked to Aachen Cathedral to pay their respects to Jesus's loincloth and swaddling clothes and to the linen cloth upon which John the Baptist's head was presented to Salome.[36] Spotting a lucrative opening, the Aachener clergy marketed sturdy, sustaining, herbed cakes to the hard-traveling pilgrims.[37]

Printen are one of those cookies that are supposed to last all the way to Easter and beyond. If yours get too hard, you can put an apple slice in the tin with them. Or, you can do as the Aacheners do: break the stale Printen up, and use the crumbs to thicken the gravy to accompany your Sauerbraten.

Recipe

PRINTEN

Ingredients for the Dough
¼ cup (45 grams) brown rock sugar or turbinado sugar
2 cups (240 grams) flour
½ teaspoon cinnamon
¼ teaspoon ginger
¼ teaspoon coriander

---

36. If there is to be a Second Coming, I imagine Jesus will have to stop by the Rhineland first to pick up his clothes: just south of Aachen, the Abbey of Prüm has his sandals, and St. Peter's Cathedral in Trier has his seamless Holy Robe.

37. Michele Kayal, "Steinhart, duftend, lecker: Kulturgut Aachener Printen," December 6, 2019, nationalgeographic.de.

¼ teaspoon allspice

¼ teaspoon aniseed (freshly ground)

⅛ teaspoon cardamom

⅛ teaspoon cloves

Pinch salt

2 teaspoons baker's ammonia

½ cup (170 grams) *Grafschafter Goldsaft Zuckerrüben Sirup* (sugar beet syrup) or British "golden syrup" or ½ cup (170 grams) wildflower honey plus 1 tablespoon molasses

1 scant cup (195 grams) white sugar

1 tablespoon finely chopped orange peel

1 tablespoon rum extract

3 tablespoons milk plus a little more for glazing

Blanched almonds for topping (optional)

Pour your brown rock sugar into a plastic sandwich bag, fold over, and seal inside another sandwich bag. Pound into crystals with a hammer.

In a large bowl, mix the pounded brown rock sugar with the other dry ingredients. Set aside.

In a small pot, heat the white sugar and sugar beet syrup (or the honey and molasses) until the sugar is dissolved. Add to the dry ingredients.

Add the milk, orange peel, and rum extract. Mix well. Dough will be stiff and sticky. Put in a greased bowl, cover with plastic or waxed cloth, and let rest in a cool place overnight.

Roll out the dough on lightly floured surface to ¼-inch thickness.

Using a butter knife, cut dough into 1½-inch by 3-inch rectangles. Place on cookie sheet one inch apart. Decorate with almonds if desired.

Brush with milk and bake at 350 F (177 C) for fifteen to twenty minutes.

Chapter Four
Paradise

When it came to the finest baking, the Egyptian wheat the Romans introduced into Germania soon surpassed the native grains in popularity. Hazelnuts, red currants, raspberries, and aniseed were already there, so some of the recipes in this book would not have looked at all strange to those Germanic tribesmen with their soap-slicked Swabian knots. Ingredients like cinnamon, nutmeg, and sugar, however, had to be fetched from the very ends of the earth.

Vizier Rekhmire probably could have told you that the cinnamon he may or may not have added to his tiger nut cakes was burned as incense as often as it was eaten, and that the ancient Egyptian phoenix, or *benu* bird, built its nest out of cinnamon sticks so it would smell good when it burst into flames. What Rekhmire probably couldn't have told you was where that cinnamon came from other than from the Land of Punt, by which he may have meant Somalia. Rekhmire would have known nothing about Sri Lanka, the island where the cinnamon trees grew, because the Puntish traders never revealed their sources to the scent-hungry Egyptians. Nor would Rekhmire have known if the *ti-sps* he burned on holy days was always "true cinnamon," *Cinnamomum verum,* or the closely related cassia or even the bark of the East African camphor tree in which the southern traders also dealt.[38]

Later Egyptians were better informed. Graeco-Roman Alexandria was a center of the spice trade and remained so throughout the Middle Ages. In Europe, confusion about where the spices came from lasted a few centuries more. Thirteenth-century Crusader Jean de Joinville, a well-traveled man for his times, believed gingerroot and cinnamon bark, along with rhubarb and aloe, were dredged from the Nile in nets after being carried downriver from Paradise.[39]

If Visigothic badass Alaric had known where peppercorns, which don't turn black until they've been baked in the sun for a few days, came from, he probably would have set out for India's Malabar coast to plunder some for himself. Instead, in 410, the chieftain demanded three thousand pounds of the stuff as a thank-you for not sacking Rome. (He got it.)

At the winter solstice feast of Saturnalia, ancient Rome's "most wonderful time of the year," people exchanged black peppercorns as tokens of friendship, a practice that mystified Pliny the Elder, who wasn't fond of the spice.[40] The educated Pliny was aware that the seeds of *Piper nigrum* came from India, but "barbarians" like Alaric probably didn't have a clue. That didn't stop them from demanding it; once the northern tribesmen had tasted pepper, homegrown juniper berries, horseradish, cumin, aniseed, and angelica stalks would no longer do for flavoring their beer, bread, and porridge. They wanted more spices, and they wanted them now.

38. Manniche, *An Ancient Egyptian Herbal*, 88.

39. Michael Krondl, *The Taste of Conquest*, 13.

40. O'Connell, *The Book of Spice*, 47.

Piper nigrum, which is still grown and harvested on the Malabar coast, is in no way related to the bell and chili peppers, members of the genus *Capsicum*, which were first cultivated in Central America. We can lay the blame for the linguistic confusion at the feet of Christopher Columbus, who brought back a load of those other peppers to prove to his sponsors at the Spanish court that he had reached the "Indies." In his defense, Columbus had probably never seen an actual pepper plant, a woody vine that wraps itself around tall trees like palms and mangos. In the end, Queen Isabella didn't buy it, and she eventually had Columbus hauled back to Spain in chains.

The new names the spices acquired on their way to the European market demonstrate the confusion about where they came from and what, exactly, they were. The *nut* in *nutmeg* is obvious, but the *meg* comes from Old French *muge*, which is from Latin *muscus* or "musky." Do Germans call nutmeg *Muskat* because of that musky aroma or because they thought it came from the city of Muskat in Oman? For a long time, nutmeg's point of origin was a well-kept secret, but by the year 1000, the nut had been cracked, so to speak, at least in the East. The Persian medical writer Ibn Sinna (known as Avicenna in Latin translation) called it *jansi ban*, "Banda nut," after the Banda archipelago where it was grown.[41] The words *nutmeg* and *mace* offer the English speaker no hint that both spices come from the same fruit, but the Germans make the connection by calling mace *Muskatblüte*, "nutmeg blossom," even though mace is not the blossom but the nutmeg seed's lacey covering.

41. O'Connell, *The Book of Spice*, 167.

As for that "counterfeit" cinnamon, cassia, its taxonomical name, *Cinnamomum aromaticum*, is redundant: the *amon* in both *cinnamon* and *cardamom* comes from an Arabic word meaning "fragrant spice."[42] The Arabs didn't grow cinnamon, but they traded in it and were instrumental in moving it along to the Egyptians, Romans, and, later, the Venetians. The Europeans were latecomers to the spice trade, and at first, they were only a small part of it. In the 1400s, most of what was grown in South Asian gardens was consumed in northern India, Persia, and China, as it had been for hundreds and probably thousands of years.[43]

Cinnamon in German is *Zimt*, but my Low German–speaking great-grandmother called it *Kanel*, probably from Italian *canella*, "little tube" or "canal." The word *cinnamon* is ultimately Semitic, coming into English from Greek via Old French, *cinnamone*, though the French now call it *cannelle*. Why two words for the same thing? I'm guessing that *canella*, which also means "little cannon," was a Venetian nickname for the little bark quills in which cinnamon comes. Instead of *canelle*, a word which probably came into fashion later, the English acquired the Old French *cinnamone*. As for *Zimt*, the German courtiers of the eighteenth century adored all things French, but, the German principalities being somewhat off the beaten track, they may not have realized the French had already switched from *cinnamone* to *cannelle*. Taking their cue from the Venetians, the Portuguese call it *canela*.

---

42. If you were hoping that *amon* might refer to Amun Re, I'm sorry to disappoint you, but the baker's *ammonia* that I insist you put in your Aachener Printen is, indeed, named for the Egyptian sun god.

43. Michael Krondl, *The Taste of Conquest*, 16.

The Venetian spice traders were happy to be identified first and foremost as businessmen, even after they were threatened with excommunication for opening offices in Muslim Alexandria, but the Portuguese traders wanted to be known as men of faith.[44] They weren't just on a quest for gold and spices, they claimed loudly in case any of the pope's spies were listening; they were also on a mission to find a lost Christian tribe. When Vasco da Gama set sail for Calcutta around the Cape of Good Hope, he had a letter addressed to Prester John in his breast pocket.[45] Prester John, whose legend arose in the twelfth century, was said to rule over an isolated Christian kingdom in either India, Mongolia, or Ethiopia. A descendant of one or all three Magi, he was supposed to be fabulously wealthy, his subjects dining off plates cut from jewels.

Vasco was never able to deliver that letter, but the Portuguese did find another source of pepper, or something like it, in Africa. The seeds of *Aframomum melegueta*, a member of the ginger family, were familiar to fifteenth-century cooks who used them just like *Piper nigrum*, adding them also to their wine and beer. (There were few spices medieval Europeans *didn't* put in their wine.) The Portuguese dominated the melegueta trade, but it was the Venetians who started calling melegueta, along with the seeds of several other sub-Saharan African herbs, "grains of Paradise."

The spice traders encouraged the idea that their goods came from an earthly Paradise because it increased their

44. Jack Turner, "The Spice That Built Venice," *Smithsonian Magazine*, November 2, 2015, https://www.smithsonianmag.com/travel /spice-trade-pepper-venice-180956856/#:~:text=And%20of%20all %20the%20spices,work%20for%20an%20unskilled%20laborer.

45. Michael Krondl, *The Taste of Conquest*, 130.

market value, made the traders look pious, and was impossible to refute. The severed heads, hands, and hearts in the reliquaries in Europe's cathedrals were said to smell like spices because the saints to which they had belonged were in *Paradise*, a word that originally meant "a walled garden." Nowadays, a whiff of cinnamon, ginger, nutmeg, and cloves tells us it's time to start hunting for a Christmas tree, but to the medieval imagination, these were the scents in the Garden of Eden.

Medieval Europeans didn't know where their spices came from, but they knew their way around a lot more of them than we do, and those early Christmas breads and cakes probably had vastly more complicated flavors than our own gingerbread or Lebkuchen. "You only have *one* kind of ginger?" the medieval cook might exclaim if he could examine even a well-stocked spice cabinet like mine. "Where is your micchino, your columbino, your zedoary? I see your pepper," he would go on, clutching his liripipe, "but where is your cubeb, your galingale, your melegueta?" A Venetian apothecary would probably have had the same reaction. Whether you had an upset stomach or you wanted to bake a cake, you would visit the *spezialo*, the "spice guy," or "specialist."

Mystical Finance

The spice trade was a risky business, even for those who remained on land. Would the ship you'd poured your savings into ever come in? And if it did, would it still have all its cargo on board? Or would it limp into port, sails drooping, holds half empty? How much an investor could charge for his share of the incoming cargo depended on how well the faraway pepper, clove, and nutmeg groves were doing and how many other ships had made it back that year. If only you had a crystal ball! Or, better yet, an astrologer.

Christopher Kurz, a Nuremberg-born astrologer working in Antwerp, claimed to be able to predict what other merchants would be charging for spices two weeks before the prices were set. Kurz specialized in pepper, saffron, and ginger, but, given the proper incentive, he would also theorize about cloves, cinnamon, and nutmeg.[46] Kurz and the other astrologers trolling the wharves and warehouses of the great spice cities could identify auspicious dates for setting sail, predict whether or not pirates would befall the ship, and cast the horoscopes of those about to embark.[47]

Kurz and his cronies were learned men. They kept detailed casebooks, corresponded eloquently with distant clients, drew up market reports, and often dabbled in the "true" sciences as well. Unlike practitioners of lower magic, they don't seem to have run afoul of the church. When one of his clients asked him how he'd acquired his gift for prognostication, Kurz said he believed that God had given it to him.[48] But were these astrologers really fortune tellers or just early economists?

Christmas in Old Bombay

For a long time, the Dutch were content to pick up their exotic prescriptions in Lisbon, and the Lisboetas were happy to supply them. But when Portugal, along with Spain, became part of

46. William Eamon, "Renaissance Astrology and the Vagaries of the Market," November 27, 2022, https://williameamon.com/renaissance -astrology-and-the-vagaries-of-markets/.

47. Brendan Dooley, *A Companion to Astrology in the Renaissance* (Boston: Brill, 2014), 161.

48. Eamon, "Renaissance Astrology and the Vagaries of the Market."

the militantly Catholic Hapsburg Empire, the Catholic Portuguese and the Protestant Dutch found themselves on opposing sides of the schism, and the Dutch were deprived of their spices. Eager to bring the heretic Hollanders to heel, Hapsburg Emperor Philip II sent an invading force to the Lowlands. Long story short, the Lowlanders trounced them, beefed up their own fleets, and set sail to grab the spices for themselves, leaving a lot of burnt Portuguese ships in their wake. The Dutch eventually took over most of the eastern routes and colonies Lisbon had once ruled, but Indian Goa remained under Portuguese control until the 1960s when it was returned to India.

For many of us, Christmas just wouldn't be Christmas without Indian ginger and cardamom. Our Christmas tastes and smells like India, but what does India look like at Christmastime? To answer this question, I turned to *Murder in Old Bombay* author Nev March, who grew up in Mumbai, a.k.a. Bombay. Nev is a Parsee, or Indian Zoroastrian. In Roman times, the priests of the Zoroastrian religion were known as magi, as in the Three Magi: Caspar, Balthasar, and Melchior. While Christmas was not part of Nev's religious heritage, it was very much part of her childhood. The Parsees are just one of several ethnic and religious minorities in Mumbai, and in the neighborhood where Nev grew up, someone was always celebrating something, Christmas following close on the heels of the Hindu Diwali festival.

In December, Christian families hung multicolored, starshaped lanterns in the alleyways, and Nev's Goan neighbors baked cookies topped with colored castor sugar. Baking in 1970s Mumbai was not as simple as turning a dial and opening a door. The oven, a square metal box with a glass front, was hauled down from the shelf only for special occasions. Positioned over a stovetop burner, it was stuffed full to make the most efficient use of the gas in the canister.

Just one of a dazzling array of sweets on offer in Goan households at Christmastime, the colorful nankhatai are probably the easiest to make. You can make them with unsalted butter, but if you use the more authentic ghee (clarified butter), which you can get at an Indian grocery store, they'll have a slightly nuttier taste.

One thing all the nankhatai recipes I consulted agreed on was that they should not contain any eggs. I wondered why, since Indian Christians may eat eggs. When I brought samples to my neighbor to try, the first thing she asked was, "Do they have eggs in them?" When I told her they didn't, she was pleased. No eggs meant that her in-laws, Hindus visiting from India, could also eat them. So perhaps the no-egg rule is to ensure that these cookies can be shared with one's Hindu neighbors. (Mine liked them and asked for the recipe. They also taught me how to pronounce the name: *NAHN-kha-tye*.)

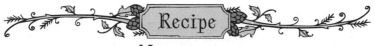

Recipe

NANKHATAI

Ingredients

½ cup (113 grams) softened unsalted butter or ½ cup (88 grams) ghee

¾ cup (85 grams) powdered sugar

2 teaspoons rose water

1 cup (120 grams) flour

¼ cup (21 grams) ladoo besan (coarsely ground chickpea
    flour)
¼ cup (40 grams) semolina flour or farina
½ teaspoon baking powder
¼ teaspoon cardamom
Chopped, unsalted pistachios or colored sugar for topping

In a large bowl, cream butter and sugar. Add rose water.

In a separate bowl, mix flours, baking powder, and cardamom. Add a little at a time to the butter mixture and work
into a smooth dough.

Roll the dough into tablespoon-sized balls.

Spread the chopped pistachios or sugar on a plate. Pat each
ball onto the plate to pick up the topping and flatten the ball
slightly. Place balls topping side up on a cookie sheet.

Bake cookies at 325 F (165 C) for ten minutes. Do not over-
bake. Nankhatai should look more white than golden.

The Good Maharajah

While we were on the phone, Nev March related to me
another Indian "Christmas story": that of the "Good Maharajah" Digvijay Singh, an almost legendary figure who had a
lot in common with that old champion of sailors and down-
on-their-luck children, St. Nicholas. In the 1940s, the Good
Maharajah made a temporary home for as many as a thousand
Polish refugee children in Nawanagar on the Arabian Sea. In
the version of the story that had been passed down to Nev,
the children were Jewish and had been turned away from port
after port before the Good Maharajah not only offered them
a safe haven but legally adopted them so they could share his
British citizenship. Each year at Christmastime, the grown

children and their descendants would gather for a reunion in Nawanagar to remember the Good Maharajah. It was a lovely story, and I wanted to know more.

At least most of the children, I learned, were not Jewish but Christian and had traveled not by boat but overland through Central Asia from the Siberian labor camps where their Polish parents had been interned. They resided in Nawanagar from 1942 to 1946, calling their benefactor "Bapu," or "father." Since the plan had always been to reunite the children with their Polish families when the war was over, I think it unlikely that Digvijay Singh would have legally adopted them. In fact, he went to great lengths to create a little Poland in Nawanagar, hiring Christian cooks from Goa and encouraging the celebration of Polish festivals, all at his own expense. At Christmas, he dressed up as St. Nicholas and distributed gifts from the backs of three camels, allaying the children's fears that the saint wouldn't be able to get his sleigh over the sands of northern India.[49]

I wasn't able to find any information about what kinds of Christmas treats those Goan cooks whipped up during the children's sojourn, but I wouldn't have been surprised if they'd baked pierniczki, Polish gingerbread. After all, they wouldn't have had to go far for the ginger!

The chewy pierniczki taste a lot like what's sold in Germany under the name *Russisches Brot*, "Russian bread," a.k.a.

---

49. You can hear a few of the surviving children tell their own stories in Sumit Osmand Shaw and Anu Radha, "A Little Poland in India (English)—The Complete Documentary," AakaarFilms, accessed January 27, 2023. https://www.youtube.com/watch?v=rIPq-8RZxxM.

German alphabet cookies.[50] I think the "Russian" in the name is for their strong honey flavor. Even back in the days of the medieval Hanseatic trading league, Russia and Poland were important sources of honey and beeswax. You can cut yours out in any shape you like.

Recipe

PIERNICZKI

Ingredients

½ cup (99 grams) sugar
½ cup (170 grams) honey
2 eggs
2½ cups (180 grams) flour plus a little more for rolling out
1 teaspoon baking soda
1 teaspoon cinnamon
1 teaspoon ginger
⅛ teaspoon cloves
1 teaspoon aniseed
Milk for brushing

In a small pot, heat the sugar and honey just until the sugar is dissolved. Let cool a bit. Beat in the eggs.

Add the dry ingredients a little at a time. Form the dough into a ball, put it in a greased bowl, and cover with plastic or a waxed cloth. Let the dough sit in a cool place at least over-

---

50. "German alphabet cookies," like American alphabet soup, are meant to teach children to read. In Austria, *Springerle*, anise-flavored cookies, were sometimes impressed with the whole alphabet for the same purpose. And according to Ashkenazi tradition, hornbooks inscribed with Hebrew letters were coated with honey, which the student was encouraged to lick off as he studied.

night. (I left mine for three days, but some Polish bakers leave theirs for a week.)

Roll the dough out to ⅛-inch thickness, cut into shapes, and put on a cookie sheet. Brush shapes with milk.

Bake cookies at 400 F (205 C) for eight to ten minutes or until golden.

If your pierniczki get hard, put a slice of bread in the tin with them. They will soften up in a few hours.

Chapter Five

St. Nicholas's Shadow

he children's festival of St. Nicholas was established in Amsterdam as early as 1360, and the *pepernoten*, "pepper nuts," that were first sold at the annual St. Nicholas Day market are probably just as old.[51] In his book *Santa Claus Worldwide*, Tom A. Jerman makes the case for the Dutch Sinterklaas and his descendant Santa Claus, both of whom bear "nicknames" derived from St. Nicholas, as almost entirely secular figures, but back in the fourteenth century, the guy credited with dropping sweets inside children's shoes was none other than St. Nicholas of Myra, a figure who came from the same vaguely imagined East as the spices.[52]

In addition to sailors, pawnbrokers, slaves, virgins, merchants, brewers, and, unofficially, the city of Amsterdam, St. Nicholas is also the patron saint of thieves. Born in the town of Myra in what is now southwestern Turkey, he returned there after studying under Egypt's Desert Fathers, was appointed bishop, and died there on December 6, 346. While his relics did indeed spend some time in his hometown of Myra, they

---

51. Michael Krondl, *The Taste of Conquest*, 190.

52. Tom A. Jerman, *Santa Claus Worldwide: A History of St. Nicholas and Other Holiday Gift-Bringers* (Jefferson, North Carolina: McFarland & Company, 2020), 11.

may have been translated there from an earlier shrine on the island of Gemile.

St. Nicholas's corpse must have been happy in Myra, because it was there that it began to produce a clear, rosy-smelling liquid everyone agreed to call "myrrh."[53] In 1087, after Myra fell to the Seljuk Turks, some Italian sailors effected a "rescue" of the saint's skull and long bones, bringing them home to the Norman-held city of Bari just north of the heel of Italy's boot. There, the bones continued to make myrrh and to inspire the eastward-bound Crusaders, who stopped to pray at the shrine on their way to and from the Holy Land.

In 1100, the Venetians undertook their own mission to Myra, muscled their way past the handful of Greek monks guarding the copper urn into which the saint's smaller bones had been gathered, and carried the relics off to the church of San Nicolo de Lido, which had already been prepared for them. Over in Bari, St. Nicholas's caretakers continue to bottle and sell the myrrh the larger bones exude, but the bones on the Lido have run dry.

Black Peter

Miniature examples of the cogs in which medieval merchants sailed the waters of the Baltic and North Seas can be seen on city coats of arms and dangling from the ceilings of St. Nicholas churches all along the coast. When the members of the Dutch East India Company set out on their voyages of murder and mayhem, it was in armed, deep-belled "East Indiaman,"

---

53. Real myrrh, as in "gold, frankincense, and myrrh," is a resin. It comes from an Arabian evergreen tree, not a human body.

but the peaceful St. Nicholas always arrives in Amsterdam by steamer.

When he appears on the eve of his feast day, St. Nicholas, or Sinterklaas, is usually accompanied by his controversial sidekick *Zwarte Piet,* "Black Peter," who tosses crunchy *kruidnoten, pepernoten,* and other sweets into the crowd. Wearing the same sixteenth-century doublet, cap, and puffy trousers that the Spanish soldiers would have worn when Phillip II sent them to subdue the heretic Hollanders, Zwarte Piet is popularly identified as a "Spanish Moor." He is, however, a caricature of a sub-Saharan African, and his current form long postdates the Catholic occupation.

Once upon a time, Zwarte Piet was probably just one of a number of devils of uncertain ethnicity who went by common male names preceded by "Black" or "Ashen" and who were no more colorful than the German Knecht Ruprecht or the Luxembourgish Houseker with his long black hair, beard, and mantle. That said, there's no evidence that Sinterklaas had a sidekick at all before 1850, a time when the Dutch sugar plantations in the Caribbean were still being worked by enslaved West Africans. The somber Houseker, who carries a bundle of twigs and sometimes a chain, is meant to inspire fear, while Zwarte Piet is more of a clown. But at whose expense is the entertainment?

At least 78 percent of the population of the South American country of Suriname, formerly Dutch Guiana, is descended from enslaved and indentured workers from India, Indonesia, and the west coast of Africa. How do the Surinamese feel about Zwarte Piet? The answer is complicated. When Suriname gained its independence from the Netherlands in 1975, the new government commuted St. Nicholas Day to

"Children's Day" and banned both Sinterklaas and Zwarte Piet from appearing in public celebrations. The dynamic duo are, however, still allowed in private spaces, and they've been making a comeback recently.[54]

Back in the "old country," Zwarte Piet remains intrinsic to the Dutch child's Christmas, but in an age when not all Dutch children are white, the idea of a white person making themself (Zwarte Piet is often played by a woman) up in blackface is problematic to say the least. One solution, which seems to be taking off in both the Netherlands and Suriname, is for *Piet* to drop the *Zwarte* and paint his face a Muppetlike purple or blue.

Recipe

PEPERNOTEN

Ingredients

¾ cup (339 grams) butter

1 cup (213 grams) packed dark brown sugar

1 egg

2¼ cups (270 grams) flour

1 teaspoon baking powder

1 teaspoon cinnamon

1 teaspoon ginger

½ teaspoon nutmeg

⅛ teaspoon cloves

---

54. Afro-Europe international blog, "Suriname abolishes Sinterklaas (and Black Pete) again," December 14, 2011, https://afroeurope.blogspot .com/2011/12/suriname-abolishes-sinterklaas-and.html.

Cream the butter and the sugar. Beat in the egg. Add the dry ingredients and work into a smooth dough.

Shape the dough into a ball and cut into quarters. Roll each quarter into a log about ten inches long. Wrap tightly in plastic and chill for at least one hour.

Cut your logs into ½-inch pieces, put the pieces on a cookie sheet, and bake at 350 F (177 C) for fifteen to twenty minutes or until lightly browned. Makes about sixty small cookies.

Mirror Images

Another Lowland Christmas tradition that has spread throughout the world is speculaas. The store-bought American versions of these cookies are shaped like windmills, but the real thing can be shaped like anything from a baroque warehouse front to a seventeenth-century lady or gentleman to St. Nicholas himself. Older molds were quite large, and the figural cookies could be as tall as American Girl dolls. The first speculaas were sweetened only or mostly with honey, making for a highly durable cookie that a child could play with, dress up, and take to bed before she ate it.

The name *speculaas* comes from the Latin word for *mirror*, because the cookie is the mirror image of the wooden mold in which the dough is pressed. Jacob Grimm theorized that such molds were originally used to make votive offerings out of dough or clay and offered to the gods in lieu of a living sacrifice.[55] While I don't doubt that such offerings were made, they were probably shaped by hand. The oldest wooden cookie molds date only to the 1500s, by which time no one in the

---

55. Jacob Grimm, *Teutonic Mythology, Volume II* (London: George Bell and Sons, 1883), 501.

lands in question was making clay or dough idols anymore—at least not openly.

Speculaas are usually store-bought, but some people do make them at home. When I emailed writer Émilie Herbert-Pontonnier to ask if she adds honey or molasses to the *speculoos*, as they're known in Belgium, that she bakes for St. Nicholas Day, she said she did not: "I think that's better for gingerbreads!" One might argue that speculoos *is* a kind of gingerbread, but the Lowland countries recognize several different kinds of speculaas/speculoos and dozens of different kinds of what you and I might simply file under "gingerbread."

Though Émilie doesn't use molasses, she insists that "brown *cassonade* is a must." It's not surprising that a Belgian would be finicky about sugar. Though Belgium is much too cold for growing sugarcane, the city of Antwerp was one of the first places in Christian Europe to further refine brown sugar into the crystalline, nearly white sugar that kings and queens desired. The sugar works at Antwerp functioned from the fourteenth century, when sugar was still a rarity, until Phillip II sacked the city.

Cassonade, or brown sugar, probably derives its name from the French *caisse*, the kind of chest in which the sugar was packed for shipment.[56] Then again, a *casson* means "a shard of glass or pottery." The most difficult characteristic of brown sugar is its tendency to turn hard as a rock when not sealed tightly enough. "Just put it in the oven with a pan of water," I was told once while crying over an impenetrable brick of brown sugar I'd left too long in a plastic bag wound with dry rubber bands. I've never had any luck with the hot water

---

56. Mintz, *Sweetness and Power*, 83.

method—only hot, hard sugar—which is why I was happy to learn the trick of putting the damp shard, or *casson*, of a terracotta flowerpot in the jar with the sugar to prevent it from hardening in the first place. (If you don't have a potsherd, you can use a slice of bread.)

The reason Émilie gives for not adding molasses or honey to her speculoos dough is that it would make the cookies too heavy. Speculoos should be "sandy," she says, and should take no more than two seconds to break when dipped in coffee.

Recipe

SPECULAAS

Ingredients
½ cup (113 grams) butter, softened
¾ cup (160 grams) brown cassonade or brown sugar
1 egg
1 teaspoon vanilla extract
2 cups (240 grams) flour
1 teaspoon baking powder
½ teaspoon cinnamon
¼ teaspoon allspice
⅛ teaspoon cloves

In a large bowl, cream the butter and brown sugar. Beat in the egg and add the vanilla.

In another bowl, mix the flour, baking powder, and spices.

Stir the flour mixture into the butter mixture. The dough will be stiff. Work the dough into a smooth ball, wrap it in plastic, and refrigerate it overnight.

Let the dough warm thirty minutes before rolling it out to ⅛-inch thickness.

Cut it into shapes and stamp with designs if desired. Put your speculaas on a cookie sheet and bake at 350 F (177 C) for twelve to fifteen minutes or until golden brown at the edges. Once you've tasted a few, let the rest sit in a tin for at least a few days.

Father Switch

Other Belgian St. Nicholas Day treats that Émilie mentioned to me are hot chocolate, tangerines, and *cougnous* (buns that might have a tiny sugar or plaster Jesus hiding inside them). Over the border in France's Alsace-Lorraine region where Émilie grew up, St. Nicholas would ride into the village on a donkey, accompanied by *le Père Fouettard*, "Father Switch." Similar in appearance to the Luxembourgish Houseker, Père Fouettard has a highly developed backstory. St. Nicholas, who seems to be the patron saint of just about everyone, proved himself a champion of children, too, when he successfully reassembled and resuscitated three little boys who had been chopped to bits by a butcher and stuffed into a pickle barrel. Or so the legend goes.

The butcher in question was none other than Père Fouettard, whom St. Nicholas assigned the bizarre penance of accompanying him on his travels and scaring the living daylights out of small children, a job Père Fouettard no doubt enjoys. Émilie recalls one St. Nicholas Day when she was five or six: Père Fouettard warned her to stop sucking her thumb or he would come back and whip her. Émilie no longer sucks her thumb, so I suppose Father Switch is doing his job.

Throw the Devil a Bone

Jacob Grimm's theory that speculaas are descended from pagan idols seems like a pretty far stretch of the rolling pin to me, especially when there are much more likely candidates, like the Rhenish *Weckmänner*—raisin-eyed, pipe-toting men made of yeast dough that migrated from St. Nicholas Day to St. Martin's Day (November 11)—or the *martini*: fancifully decorated man-on-horse cookies that are handed out to children on St. Martin's Day in Venice.

The glazed, oversized, diamond-shaped cake in the foreground of Jan Steen's c. 1665 painting *The Feast of St. Nicholas*, now in Amsterdam's Rijks Museum, is a duivekater, a sweet yeast bread similar to but not as rich as the Venetian pandoro.[57] The one in the painting is rather abstract, but a duivekater is supposed to be shaped like a bone—one of the saint's stolen, myrrh-producing long bones, perhaps? The name *duivekater* means "devil's cat," so there's a possibility that the cake is descended from one that was once offered to a god, all pagan gods being either demoted to devils or promoted to saints with the coming of Christianity.

Did the duivekater take the place of an actual cat or something larger? The name suggests a kinship with the *lussekatter*, "Lucy cat," a sweet yeast bun baked in Sweden to

---

57. Dr. Wendy Schaller, "Jan Steen, The Feast of St. Nicholas," Khan Academy, accessed September 28, 2022, https://www.khanacademy.org/humanities /renaissance-reformation/baroque-art1/holland/a/jan-steen-feast-of-st -nicholas. The fancy pastries presented in *The Feast of St. Nicholas* would not have been baked at home; that was the province of professionals like *The* [heavily muscled] *Baker Arent Oostwaard and His Wife, Catharina Keizerswaard*, who can be seen posing with a skinnier duivekater in an earlier painting of Steen's, also in the Rijks Museum.

celebrate St. Lucy's Day (December 13), the date on which, in the old Julian calendar, the winter solstice fell. Lucy cats are flavored with cardamom, duivekater with lemon peel, and sometimes cardamom and nutmeg. Lucy cats come in a variety of shapes, including a "goat," a "virgin's crown," and a "shepherd's star," but no cat. Up in Scandinavia, the goddess Freya rode in a cart pulled by cats. St. Nicholas is usually pictured riding a white horse, but there is a Holy Monastery of St. Nicholas of the Cats on the southern tip of Cyprus.

The cats were imported to Cyprus from Egypt by the future saint Helena in 328 to control a plague of snakes. The future saint Nicholas was still alive at the time, so, if the story is true, the cats preceded the monastery. I'm not sure which is less likely, that a traveling Dutchman should have brought the story of St. Nicholas's cats back to Amsterdam and named a pastry for them—one that eventually made its way to Sweden—or that the Vikings would have brought their solstice buns down to Amsterdam. And then there is the problem of that suspiciously large bone.

All duivekater are loaves with lines scored in them, some looking more like actual bones, others less so. Some are fancy, others plain. One form bears a striking resemblance to the "Wagon Wheels," one of the traditional Swedish lussekatter shapes. (See Saffron in chapter 11.) I have tried to make my duivekater look like the one in Steen's 1658 painting.

Recipe

DUIVEKATER

Ingredients

4½ cups (540 grams) flour

One .25-ounce package (7 grams) active dry yeast

½ cup (99 grams) sugar
½ teaspoon cardamom
¼ teaspoon nutmeg
1 teaspoon lemon zest
1 cup (236 milliliters) milk
½ cup (113 grams) butter plus a little more for greasing bowl
2 whole eggs

Glaze
1 egg yolk
1 tablespoon sugar

In a large bowl, mix 1½ cups flour with yeast, sugar, cardamom, nutmeg, and lemon zest.

In a small pot, heat the milk and butter just until the butter is melted. Do not let it boil. Let cool a minute before adding to the flour mixture.

Stir in the whole eggs.

Stir in another 1½ cups flour.

Turn the dough onto a floured surface and knead in the rest of flour—about a cup.

Knead for ten minutes.

Shape the dough into a ball, put it in a greased bowl, and cover the top with a damp dish towel. Let the dough rise in a warm place for one hour.

Punch the dough down and let it rest for ten minutes.

Roll the dough out gently into a long, skinny diamond, cover it with a damp towel, and let it rise for forty-five minutes.

Use a sharp knife to score deep lines in the diamond as shown in Figure 5a.

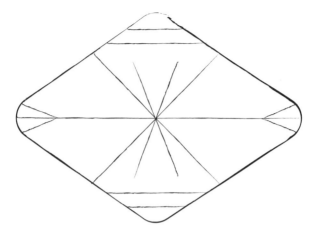

Figure 5a: Duivekater pattern

Beat the egg yolk and brush it over the diamond. Sprinkle with sugar.

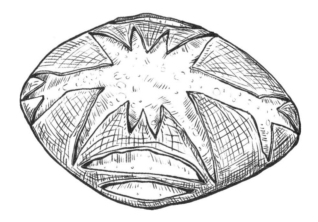

Bake your duivekater at 350 F (177 C) for forty-five minutes or until golden. Turn the oven off and leave it in for another five minutes. Slice and eat warm with coffee or toasted and buttered the next day for breakfast.

Dark Legacy of the VOC

Portuguese ships weren't the only things the Dutch burned. The officers of the *Vereenigde Oost-Indische Compagnie* (the Dutch East India Company) set fire to whole groves of cinnamon in Ceylon (Sri Lanka) and cloves in the Moluccas to keep supply from exceeding demand and to prevent those who grew the spices from selling their crops to the Company's competitors. They also went to great and violent lengths to make sure no seedlings left the territories they controlled, so I wasn't surprised to learn of the slaughter of thousands along the fiery trail blazed by the VOC. What surprised me was the fact that I'd never heard these stories before.

Because most of the history of the Dutch East India Company, and the atrocities committed in its name, has been published only in Dutch and Indonesian, the more brutal episodes remain largely unknown to the wider world and even to most Dutch people today. This has been gradually changing thanks to books like Giles Milton's *Nathaniel's Nutmeg*, Michael Krondl's *The Taste of Conquest*, Amitav Ghosh's *The Nutmeg's Curse*, and Histori Bersama, a group that has been gathering, translating, and publishing information that sheds light on the Dutch colonial past.

American high school students learn about the transatlantic slave trade and the Haitian Revolution, but few have ever heard of the nutmeg island of Banda where, late one May night in 1621, a fallen lamp startled the twitchy Dutch governor into setting fire to the village of Lontor. Those villagers who were unable to escape into the hills or nearby islands were cut down, while the *Orankaya* (resident chiefs) and other Bandanese higher-ups were drawn and quartered, their heads impaled on bamboo stakes. When it was all over, only four hundred eighty of an original Bandanese population of around fourteen thousand remained on the island.[58]

Four years after the massacre on Banda, Governor Sonck, who had set the killing in motion, drowned off the coast of Formosa (Taiwan). A year after that, Jan Pieterszoon Coen, who had led the conquest of the island, died of either cholera or dysentery in the Dutch colonial capital of Batavia (Jakarta), besieged at that time by the Javanese Sultan Agung of Mataram.[59] The Dutch won that one, too, and the VOC paid for Coen to be buried in style in the heart of the town. His tomb has since been subsumed by modern Jakarta's *Wayang* (Puppet) Museum.[60]

Today, nutmeg, cinnamon, and cloves are grown and traded far from the former Dutch East Indies. The Caribbean nation of Grenada even has a nutmeg on its flag. To the ghosts of Sonck, Coen, and the other men who stopped at nothing to maintain the VOC's stranglehold on the spices, I would ask, "How's that working for you?"

---

58. Hendri F. Isnaeni, "The VOC Genocide," April 5, 2010, http://historibersama.com/the-voc-genocide-historia/.

59. Michael Krondl, *The Taste of Conquest*, 236.

60. I found, in the Wikipedia entry for the royal burial complex of Imogiri where Sultan Agung now lies, a tantalizing reference to "a persistent folklore" that Coen's bones were stolen from his tomb in Batavia (now Jakarta) and irreverently reinterred under the steps to the complex at Imogiri. The source cited is a 1977 Indonesian language book, *Sultan Agung Hanyokrokusumo o, raja terbesar Kerajaan Mataram abad ke-17: catatan dari Imogiri* (which Google Translate tells me means "Sultan Agung Hanyakrokusumo, the greatest king of the seventeenth-century Mataram Kingdom: notes from Imogiri") by Pranata Ssp.

Chapter Six
The Bitter and the Sweet

storehouse full of sugar, a storehouse full of almonds. The inhabitants of the city of Lübeck in what was then the Holy Roman Empire were in the midst of a famine (or maybe it was a siege) when it occurred to the merchants (or maybe it was the Bürgermeister) to grind the almonds, mix them with the sugar, and distribute the loaves to the starving townsfolk. As a child, I didn't have any reason to doubt the story my mother told me about the invention of marzipan. After all, she'd grown up in Lübeck, and I'd seen those medieval brick storehouses for myself when we'd gone back to visit. She'd also told me that Lübeck's walls had been built to protect the city from the Danes, as she'd been taught in school. But while the Lübeckers did later do battle with the Danes, the fortifications were first erected to protect the invading Teutonic Knights' business interests from the natives.

Not all medieval crusades were directed at the Muslims; 1147 saw the launch of the first of several "northern crusades." In the crosshairs were the Wends, Abotrites, Pomeranians, Prussians, Lusatians, Sambians, and other pagan tribes. Armed with a papal bull, the Christian Saxons used missionary zeal as an excuse to make a play for the timber, honey, beeswax, and, along the coasts, amber, which made the Baltic and Slavic pagan territories so desirable.[61] The land grab was accomplished neither tidily nor in one fell swoop, but by the early thirteenth century, Lübeck had become the "Queen of the Hanseatic League," an alliance of merchants with offices in hundreds of cities, including Bremen, Hamburg, Bergen, Bruges, and Thorn.

Lübeck is now a UNESCO World Heritage Site, and Lübecker marzipan is famous throughout the world, but Lübeck is not the birthplace of marzipan. And those yellow brick storehouses were for keeping salt from the Lüneburg Heath, not sugar and almonds, neither of which are native to northern Europe. By the time the pointed rooftops of Lübeck's famous gate, the Holstentor, had risen to pierce the gray northern sky, marzipan was already a thousand years old.

The Wicked Drug

There are several different species of sugarcane, the most familiar of which is *Saccharum officinalis*. Sugar, which wasn't made completely white until the sixteenth century, was used both as a binding ingredient in the electuaries and syrups in which other drugs were taken, and as a drug itself.

The English word sugar comes from Arabic sakkar, (also transliterated as sukkar, as in Tawahin es-Sukkar, an early sugar-processing site near the Dead Sea) via Persian and

---

61. Alan Palmer, *The Baltic: a New History of the Region and Its People* (Woodstock, New York: The Overlook Press, 2006), 39. The Saxons' own conversion at the hands of Charlemagne a few centuries earlier had also been, for the most part, by the sword.

ultimately Sanskrit carkará, meaning "gravel."[62] The English word candy came via the same linguistic route and originally denoted sugarcane.[63] The first written reference to sugar comes from the fourth-century-BCE Sanskrit grammar *Mahābhāshya*, which mentions barley porridge, rice pudding, and a kind of flat ginger ale which were all sweetened with semirefined sugar.[64] Why a grammar should be talking about desserts, I have no idea. Maybe its author, the revered scholar Patañjali, realized how boring grammars can be and thought a spoonful of sugar references might help the lesson go down.

In Homer's *Odyssey*, the *pharmakeutria*, or "pharmacist witch," Circe serves Odysseus's crew a porridge made of barley, wine, honey, cheese, and "wicked drugs" to turn them into swine.[65] Could Circe, a character with cultural links to both Indian and Mesopotamian tradition, have also put some sugar in her magic porridge? Coastal India and the Tigris-Euphrates river delta were early centers of sugar production, and where there is cultural exchange, there is usually material exchange, too, so I wouldn't be surprised if a little Indian rock sugar made it into Circe's pantry on the island of Aeaea.

The first "prescription" for sugar comes from the c. 50 BCE medical handbook *De Materia Medica*, where it is recommended for stomach and bladder problems. The book's author mentions that sugar came from India and "Arabia Felix," i.e.,

62. Graham Chandler, "Sugar, Please," Aramco World Volume 63 Number 4, July /August 2012, https://archive.aramcoworld.com/issue/201204/sugar.please.htm.

63. Online Etymology Dictionary, "candy," accessed January 23, 2023, https://www .etymonline.com/word/candy.

64. Mintz, *Sweetness and Power*, 19.

65. Homer, *The Odyssey*, trans. Robert Fagles (New York: Viking, 1996), 237.

southern Arabia, the same source as frankincense. As late as the 1600s, one of the many English terms for sugar was *salt of Arabia Felix*.[66]

Sugar all but disappeared from Europe during the Dark Ages, not reappearing until the great Muslim expansion that started in the seventh century. By the eighth century, the first sugar refineries in the Mediterranean had been set up in Jordan and Egypt near Alexandria. In Europe, the idea of separating savory from sweet and leaving the sweet for last was an alien concept, the word *dessert* not coming into the English language until the seventeenth century. At that time, it had nothing to do with deserving; *dessert* comes from the French *desservir*, "to unserve, or clear the table."[67] In the Middle East, however, the presentation of sweets after dinner was a time-honored method of telling one's guests to get a move on. The classification of sugar and honey as pharmaceuticals was also an Arab concept, inherited, in part, from the ancient Greeks. German marzipan, Italian torrone, and Indian jalebis (a fried, sugar-soaked sweet eaten during Diwali, the Hindu Festival of Lights) may not have been invented in Baghdad, seat of the Abbasid Caliphate, but they were certainly refined in that tenth-century center of haute cuisine, and it was in their Abbasid forms that they wended their way east to India and west to Sicily, Spain, and the rest of Europe.[68]

66. Mintz, *Sweetness and Power*, 231.

67. Livia Gershon, "The Invention of Dessert," August 23, 2019, . https://daily.jstor .org/the-invention-of-dessert/.

68. Rachel Laudan, "Crossroads and Diaspora: A Thousand Years of Islamic Cuisines," Aramco World Volume 65 No. 6, November/December 2014, https:// archive.aramcoworld.com/issue/201406/crossroads.and.diasporas.a.thousand .years.of.islamic.cuisines.htm.

Sugar was not unknown in Christian Europe before 1200, but it was a luxury that appeared only, amid much pomp, at the boards of kings and queens. Crusaders returning from Muslim lands told tales of tabletop castles made of marzipan and of sugar molded into trees and, surprisingly for a Muslim court, human figures. In the late thirteenth century, the Knights of Malta grew sugarcane in the short-lived Christian Kingdom of Jerusalem, without much success. If Europeans wanted sugar, they had to get it from Arab traders.

Sugarcane was planted in Muslim Spain as early as 760, at which time it was already growing in Egypt, North Africa, Sicily, and Cyprus. Compared to the ceaseless manpowered sugar mills the Europeans would later establish in the Caribbean, Arab sugar production looks like a cottage industry, but they, too, relied on slave labor. Nine hundred years before West African slaves drove the French from the sugar-producing island of Haiti, the East African war captives who grew, harvested, and processed sugarcane in the Tigris-Euphrates delta rose up against their Arab overlords.[69]

Sugarcane waits for no man: it grows quickly, peaks quickly, and ferments quickly if it isn't cut. It also dies quickly if it doesn't get enough water, and the Arabs' desire to grow water-loving sugarcane in their own arid empire spurred a host of agricultural innovations.[70] Growing sugarcane is tricky, and processing it was both time sensitive and laborious. As it turned out, the Arabs paved the way to large-scale sugar production in more ways than one: the first slaves to be brought

69. Mintz, *Sweetness and Power*, 27.

70. Chandler, "Sugar, Please."

to the Caribbean were probably those already versed in the old Arab methods of sugarcane cultivation and processing.[71]

The price of sugar in Europe was still high when the cane fields and kettles of Sicily and Cyprus were abandoned for the tropical islands to the west where sugarcane was much happier. Better growing conditions meant more plantations, which meant increased production, lower prices, and increased demand, which the colonial powers met by enslaving a huge unpaid workforce from West Africa. The islands of the Caribbean might look like paradises to those who vacation on them today, but for the men and women who harvested the cane and boiled the sugar on the plantations, it was hell.

Sugarplums

Though the Romans managed to plant sweet almond trees (*Prunus dulcis*) as far north as Britain, they fruited only occasionally. Almond trees did much better in the milder climate of Germany's Rhineland-Palatinate, where almonds were a major export from the fifteenth through the sixteenth centuries. The region's princes, in an effort to keep the price high, restricted how many trees their subjects could cultivate.[72] It didn't take the Europeans long to catch on to the Middle Eastern idea of putting almonds and imported sugar together. The "sugarplums" that dance in the nestled children's heads in Clement Clark Moore's *'Twas the Night Before Christmas* aren't plums; they're candy-coated almonds and seeds. (Then again, in a way, they *are* plums: the genus name *Prunus* comes from the Greek word for *plum*.) Called comfits in England,

71. Mintz, *Sweetness and Power*, 30.

72. Metzger, *Culinaria Germany*, 298.

these late-medieval sweets were made by a process known as *dragée*, in which nuts and seeds were swirled laboriously in a shallow pan until they had picked up a hard sugar shell.

The pastel comfits we know as Jordan almonds first appeared in Italy in the 1300s, along with the dragée method.[73] The ancient Romans were already handing out honeyed almonds at major life events, as we now give out little bags of Jordan almonds, though few of us actually eat them. It may be only coincidence that the first sugar processing plants in the Middle East were in the Jordan Valley—Jordan almonds were probably named for the Jordan River along whose banks almond trees grew. Then again, *Jordan* may come from the French *jardin*, "garden," as in the Garden of Eden.

Jordan almonds are made with sweet almonds, the same kind that make up most of a loaf of marzipan. A tiny part of marzipan, however, is *Prunus dulcis*'s evil daughter, *Prunus amara*, the bitter almond. Bitter almonds, which are so bitter that no one would ever be tempted to eat them by the handful, contain the chemical compound amygdalin, the source of marzipan's signature flavor. If you *did* manage to eat a whole handful of bitter almonds, it would be your last: amygdalin is also the source of cyanide.

It would be interesting to know how many bodies ended up on the kitchen floor while those early confectioners were figuring out how much bitter almond oil they could safely add to a loaf of marzipan, but by the time Muslim scholars started writing the recipes down, it had all been sorted out. Ibn Sayyan al-Warraq's *Book of Dishes*, written in Baghdad in the

73. Metro Creative. "The story behind Jordan almonds," Richmond-Times Dispatch, June 29, 2014, https://richmond.com/the-story-behind-jordan-almonds /article_00c20dfa-fd5c-11e3-8165-001a4bcf6878.html.

late tenth century, includes recipes for fifty different sweets, including marzipan.[74] Italy's marzipan industry started out in Sicily, where ground almonds and sugar were flavored with orange flower water. The art of making and modelling marzipan, which Sicilian nuns took over from Sicily's first Arab confectioners, continues on the island today. As in Lübeck, marzipan fruits are a favorite theme, but back in the Middle Ages, the subjects were more often religious. In the 1600s, a favorite shape of the marzipan-making sisters was "Virgin's breasts" topped with glacé cherries.[75]

The English word *marchpane*, "marzipan," was still the preferred term in 1960, the year my Webster's dictionary was published. *Marchpane* derives ultimately from Latin *panis*, "bread," and *marsa*, "frumenty," a sweet porridge of sprouted wheat and almond milk that was eaten in the Middle Ages at Christmastime.[76] Or do both the English and the German words descend from Arabic *manthaban*, a little box in which marzipan was kept or in which the almonds and sugar were measured?[77] Then again, the name may come from the word *mawthaban*, "seated king." An image of a seated king appeared on a Byzantine coin of the same name that was circulated in eleventh-century Toledo and used to stamp the marzipan

---

74. Laudan, "Crossroads and Diaspora."

75. Claudia Piras, *Culinaria Italy: Pasta, Pesto, Passion*, trans. Giorgio Sinigalia (Rheinbreitbach, Germany: H. F. Ullmann, 2004), 446.

76. A Dollop of History, "Frumenty, A Medieval Wheat Porridge," March 15, 2020, https://historydollop.com/2020/03/15/frumenty-a-medieval-wheat-porridge/. Article includes a fourteenth-century recipe for "Furmente wt Porpays." Yes, "porpays." As in "porpoise."

77. Piras, *Culinaria Italy*, 446.

loaves before they were baked. Or so the story goes.[78] Spanish Christians were already eating such loaves at Christmastime under Muslim rule, and to this day, Toledano confectioners impress their marzipan with designs—in a wooden mold, though, not with a coin—before they brush it with egg yolk and bake it.

The German confectioners got their sugar from the Venetians, who, by the late Middle Ages, had their own sugar plantations on Cyprus and Crete. Closer to hand was the other principal ingredient of marzipan: Rhenish almonds. As Queen of the Hanseatic League, Lübeck was well placed to launch her own marzipan industry, though when exactly she did so isn't clear. Today, there are several brands of Lübecker marzipan, all of which feature that famous gate, the Holstentor, on their labels. Lübecker marzipan is less sweet than other varieties, and the Niederegger brand, which is the least sweet of all, has a very faint greenish cast to it. Lübecker marzipan is flavored with rose water instead of orange flower water, and the apples,

---

78. Tor Eigeland, "Arabs, Almonds, Sugar, and Toledo," Aramco World April/June 1996 Volume 47 Number 3, April/June 1996, https://archive.aramcoworld.com /issue/199603/arabs.almonds.sugar.and.toledo.htm. But I'm not sure we should let Eigeland have the last word. According to University of Santa Cruz linguistics professor Pranav Anand, who was curious about the marzipan in his wedding cake, the coin in question was a Venetian-struck *mataban*, and the seated king was Christ on his throne. While Eigeland pooh-poohs the idea that marzipan comes from *marci panis*, "St. Mark's bread," Anand puts forward the idea that it may have been derived from *Martius panis*, "bread of Mars," Mars being the Roman god of war, since marzipan was often used to make models of fortified castles. (See Pranav Anand, "Anand/Vamosi Wedding," What's Happening at Santa Cruz? September 24, 2007, https://whascling.sites.ucsc.edu/2007/09/.) Anand doesn't include any pictures in his piece, which is really just a wedding announcement, but Eigeland includes one of an antique wooden mold showing Toledo's fortified Bisagra Gate.

oranges, peaches, and bananas are more subtly shaded than their bright, glossy Italian counterparts.

The Niederegger company's website readily traces marzipan's origins to tenth-century Persia, not to a local famine or siege, which brings us to yet another, more probable etymology.[79] The Persian word *mazupan* sounds a lot more like *marzipan* than any of the other contenders. *Mazupan*, meaning "high honcho," more or less, alludes to a time when comfits and electuaries were available only to the elite. In today's Middle East, marzipan seems to have ceded its place to halwa, the most familiar of which is made with sesame seed paste, but Arabs do still eat sweet almond paste under its name of *halwa al-marzuban*, "the elite sweet."[80]

Whoever named it, marzipan was a sweet way of circumventing the Advent fast, but even after the imperial free city of Lübeck became Protestant, marzipan was reserved for Christmas.[81] This was still the state of affairs in 1806 when Johann Georg Niederegger, who had migrated from the city of Ulm in southern Germany, took over Lübeck's Maret Confectionary. Hitting on a winning and highly secret formula involving less sugar and more almonds, he opened a bigger shop opposite the stone staircase of Lübeck's Gothic town hall. By this time, the process of extracting sugar from native sugar beets had been developed, which meant that Germans didn't have to rely on imported sugar. Now that marzipan was no longer an expensive seasonal treat, Niederegger began molding it into

79. Niederegger, "History of Marzipan," accessed January 24, 2023, https://www .niederegger.de/en/marzipan/history-of-marzipan/.

80. Eigeland, "Arabs, Almonds, Sugar, and Toledo."

81. Germany's "imperial free cities" answered only to the Holy Roman Emperor.

everyday shapes—there's a Niederegger red squirrel (*Sciuris vulgaris*) watching over my shoulder as I write.

The original Niederegger Café was bombed in 1942 and rebuilt on the same spot in 1948. The market downstairs remains a bustling place where shoppers pile marzipan fruits, mammals, herrings, and starfish into metal baskets along with the classic "white" (plain) and "black" (dark chocolate–covered) loaves. In Germany, a pink marzipan pig is a good luck token, especially at New Year's, but this tradition, too, originated in Sicily where marzipan pigs are eaten, or at least bought, for St. Sebastian's Day (January 20).

Several years ago, on a visit to northern Germany, my relations and I paused beside the road leading to the heart of the reconstructed Viking town of Haithabu to consume a little bag of marzipan potatoes. We'd just walked a significant stretch of the Danevirke, the earthworks erected by the Danes to keep out the Franks, and we were in need of some sustaining.[82] A discussion ensued about whether or not it was appropriate be to eating marzipan potatoes outside a Viking town, since potatoes, a New World food, were never part of the Viking diet. In the end, we decided it was entirely appropriate. Having no access to genuine specimens of *Solanum tubersosum*, marzipan potatoes would have been the only kind of potatoes available to the Vikings.[83]

---

82. I'm not sure what relationship, if any, those northern Franks have to the Franks now living in and around Nuremberg.

83. No, of course, the Vikings didn't eat marzipan potatoes. They didn't know what a potato was. They probably didn't know what marzipan was, either, though those who worked their way east to Byzantium may have seen it. The Haithabuans had no almond trees, but they did have peach trees, from which they could have made a second-rate persipan, I suppose, but I doubt they had the skill, let alone the sugar. For more about what the Haithabuans *did* eat, see my article "The Golden Apples of Jotunheim" in Llewellyn's 2013 *Herbal Almanac*.

I don't have the skill to shape and color a grinning marzipan pig or faintly blushing marzipan peach, but marzipan potatoes, another favorite "subtlety" of the Germans, are a breeze.

Recipe

MARZIPAN POTATOES

Ingredients

1 batch homemade marzipan or 1 cup (about 300 grams) store-bought marzipan

¼ cup (11 grams) unsweetened cocoa powder

If your marzipan has been in the refrigerator, leave it out for a few minutes to warm up. If it's too sticky to roll into a ball, leave it unwrapped for a few minutes to half an hour to dry, but keep checking on it. You don't want it to get so dry that it will crumble.

When the marzipan's ready, pinch off a tablespoon-sized amount, roll it into a ball, and prick it here and there with a pointed toothpick. You can dent it with a butter knife, too, to make it look less like a ball and more like a potato. Put your cocoa powder in a bowl and roll your potatoes around in it one at a time. Brush off the excess powder and set the potatoes aside to dry a little before packing or giving them away.

Colorful Plates

"Then I put the plate out. Nicholas will for sure leave something on it," is the gist of a line from the traditional St. Nicholas Day carol "Lasst uns froh und munter sein" ("Let's be happy and lively"), made famous throughout Germany when Heribert and Johannes Grüger included it in their book of children's songs, *Die Liederfiebel*, in 1930. How you get your St. Nicholas Day treats depends on what part of Germany you're from. In Lübeck, children put out shoes, not plates, for the saint to fill as he passes by. As a child, my mother was under the impression that it was St. Nicholas's companion, the gloomy Knecht Ruprecht, who would put sweets in her shoe if she was good, a lump of coal or a birch switch if she was bad. (She was never bad.) Because she never saw either of them, she made no distinction between St. Nicholas and his somber helper, at least not until she got to school and had to memorize Theodor Storm's lengthy poem "Knecht Ruprecht."

On Christmas Eve, the red-robed *Weihnachtsmann*, "Christmas Man," arrived to deliver the presents, or at least to signal to the children that it was time to open the packages hidden under the white sheet under the candlelit tree. My mother was terrified of the Weihnachtsmann until she realized it was her best friend's father in costume. For her, the best part of Christmas Eve was the presentation of the *bunter Teller*. On Advent Sundays, a plate of cookies was set on the table for everyone to take from, but on Christmas, each child got their own "colorful plate," a fluted cardboard dish printed with Christmas designs. The ones my mother remembers held marzipan potatoes, those Pfefferkuchen "cobblestones," and the molasses-flavored "brown" Pfefferkuchen, with an apple or an orange in the center of the plate. Star-shaped Pfefferkuchen with a hole cut in the middle could be either eaten right away or hung on the Christmas tree. Crispy when they came out of the oven, they would be soft by the time the tree came down on New Year's Day.

Indian Christians have a similar tradition in the *consoada*, a platter of homemade Christmas cookies and confections presented to guests and neighbors. The consoada is inspired in part by the Portuguese tradition of sending Christmas care packages to those who have suffered some misfortune and who need "consoling," and in part by the basket of sweets a Hindu bride's family was expected to send to the groom's family for the couple's first Diwali.[84]

Because the platters are presented on the occasion of Jesus's birth, this tradition reminded me of an ornately painted Italian platter I'd seen at the Metropolitan Museum of Art and that, according to its label, had been filled with sweets and presented to a mother after she had given birth.[85] Such a platter, I learned later, was most often presented after the birth of a son. Of course, only the very wealthy could afford to commission a *desco da parto* (birth salver), as the platter was called, but large families were as valued among the rich as they were among the poor, and in the Middle Ages, both groups suffered from high percentages of infant mortality, so every live birth was a cause for celebration.[86] Goa was a Portuguese colony, not an Italian one, but I can't help wondering if the consoada could be, at least partly, an echo of this medieval Italian tradition.

84. Celina de Vieira Velho e Almeida, "The Christmas Consoada In Goa: Its Origin," December 18, 2019, https://www.heraldgoa.in/Goa/The-Christmas-Consoada -In-Goa-Its-Origin/154833.

85. Metropolitan Museum of Art, "Birth Tray (Desco da Parto) with the Triumph of Chastity (recto) and Naked Boys with Poppy Pods (verso) c. 1450–60," accessed January 24, 2023, https://www.metmuseum.org/art/collection/search/479708.

86. Jacqueline Marie Musacchio, "The Medici-Tornaburi *Desco da Parto* in Context." *Metropolitan Museum Journal*, Volume 33 (1998), *JSTOR*, 137, https://www .journals.uchicago.edu/doi/10.2307/1513010.

Among the sweets that should be on the Goan consoada platter are the nankhatai we made in chapter 4 and colored fruits molded from a marzipanlike cashew paste. Is there a connection between the consoada and the bunter Teller? Probably not. The bunter Teller tradition dates only to the nineteenth century—the first plain paper plate was invented by a Brandenburger bookbinder in 1867.[87] Fifteen or so Christmases later, children all over Germany were eating cookies off paper plates printed with stars, candles, and Christmas roses. The tradition arrived just in time: by the late eighteenth century, Christmas trees were going up in almost all German homes, the bunter Teller arriving just in time to distract the kids from the burning candles.

Craft

STAR-SHAPED COOKIE TRAY

Tools and Materials

Matte-finish Christmas wrapping paper (glossy paper doesn't glue well)

Small (about 2¾-inch or 38½-centimeter) square of cardboard

Pencil

Scissors

Glue

---

87. Karen Lodder, "What Is a Bunter Teller? A Plate of Christmas Cookies for Everyone!" German Girl in America, December 12, 2016, https://germangirlinamerica .com/what-is-a-bunter-teller/#:~:text=Bunter%20Teller%20translates%20as%20 %E2%80%9Ccolorful,that%20is%20given%20at%20Christmas.

Trace a dinner plate on a sheet of paper and cut out.

Fold the circle into sixteenths. Unfold to quarters, plain side out, and draw and cut out the points as shown (Figure 6a).

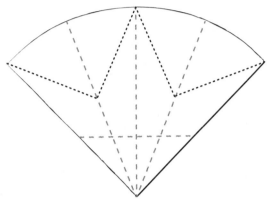

Figure 6a

Fold the bottom up (Figure 6b). Unfold.

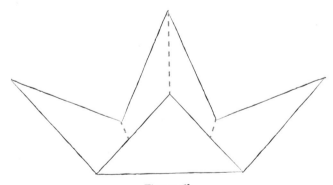

Figure 6b

Sharpen all creases.

Glue and pinch the eight points with the printed side of the paper inside. When the points are dry, push the bottom down flat (Figure 6c).

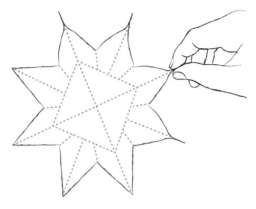

Figure 6c

Glue a square of cardboard to the underside of the dish (Figure 6d) and fill with small cookies and marzipan potatoes (Figure 6e).

Figure 6d

Figure 6e—Final cookie tray

King's Mountain Marzipan

Like Lübeck, the city of *Königsberg*, "king's mountain," at the far eastern end of the Baltic Sea was established by the monastic military Order of Teutonic Knights, who built their fortress on top of the Sambian town that was already there. The Teutonic Knights were as interested in the region's wheat, furs, honey, and amber as they were in saving pagan souls, and the city soon became a hub of trade as well as the venue for crowning Prussian kings. From 1255 until 1945, Königsberg's lingua franca was German, and it was here that E. T. A. Hoffmann was born. Hoffmann was the author of the 1816 short story "The Nutcracker and the Mouse King," which inspired *The Nutcracker*, a Christmas ballet that is defined, appropriately, by sweetmeats.

After World War II, Königsberg became Kaliningrad, and any ethnic Germans who had not already fled the bombed-out city were deported west, the confectioners among them bringing with them their molds and unique recipe for filled, toasted marzipan. Königsberger marzipan isn't shaped into fruits and animals, and it's never colored. Instead, the marzipan is rolled out and pressed into loaves, lozenges, coils, and rings.

The pagan Sambians, speakers of an archaic branch of Indo-European that's still spoken in Latvia and Lithuania today, were more than simple forest dwellers. Sambian aristocrats, known in archaeological circles as the "amber elites," were laid to rest with bronze vessels, bracelets, and brooches adorned with indented rings and coiled wires.[88] Do the traditional Königsberger marzipan shapes reflect this heritage? Sadly, no; the art of marzipan-making came fairly late to Königsberg, and the first confectioners to set up shop were from various points in Central Europe. Still, that doesn't mean we can't think of the fallen amber elites when we make our *Näpfchen*, "little ring cakes."

The Näpfchen are one of the easiest filled shapes to make, and you can do it without a mold. After the Näpfchen are toasted, the filling—jam, icing, or chocolate—is piped or dropped in. The quintessential Christmas Näpfchen is filled with white icing and topped with chopped pistachios and maraschino cherries, but other nuts, fruits, and even candied angelica stalks have also been used.

---

88. Viktoria Greenboim Rich, "The 'Amber Elites' in Ancient Kaliningrad Went to Eternity With Their Horses," Haaretz/Archaeology. December 28, 2021, https://www.haaretz.com/archaeology/2021-12-28/ty-article/the-amber-elites-in-ancient-kaliningrad-went-to-eternity-with-their-horses/0000017f-dc08-d3ff-a7ff-fda861510000.

Königsberger Marzipan

Ingredients for the Little Cakes

1 batch homemade marzipan or 1 cup (about 300 grams)
  store-bought marzipan
Powdered sugar

Tools

Shot glass or plastic medicine dosing cup
Plastic soda bottle cap
Round toothpick

For Christmas Filling

½ cup (56 grams) powdered sugar
2 ½ teaspoons lemon juice
A few maraschino cherries, cut up and left to dry for an hour
  or more
A handful of pistachios, chopped

**Other Fillings (one or more of the following,
a few tablespoons of each)**

Apricot jam
Seedless raspberry jam
Nutella

Dust your work surface with powdered sugar. Roll out the
marzipan to ¼-inch thickness. (If it's been in the refrigerator,
let it warm up for half an hour.)

Cut out circles with the shot glass. Press the soda bottle cap, open side up, in the center of each circle to form a rim around the edge of each circle. Don't go all the way through!

Use the pointed end of a round toothpick to make indentations all around the rim of each cake. Place the cakes on a parchment-lined cookie sheet. (They won't expand, so you can put them close together.)

Stir down the jams until they're smooth.

Put the cakes in the broiler and turn the oven dial to the broiler setting. Broil them for three minutes, give or take. Keep an eye on them! Once the rims turn brown, you won't have long to pull them out before they turn black.

Fill the ones you want to fill with jam or Nutella as soon as they come out of the oven—a tiny spoonful in each.

Let the others cool while you're making the icing and chopping the pistachios (your cherries should already be cut up and drying). Spoon the icing into the cooled cakes and add the toppings. Let them dry several hours before putting them in a tin. Makes about twenty-four.

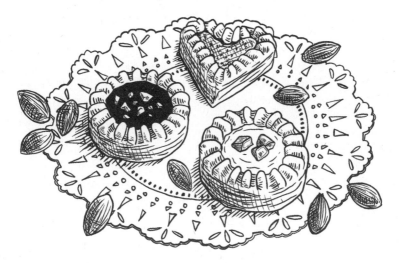

Marzipan Heraldry

The confectioners in Baghdad, Alexandria, and Damascus bound crystalline sugar with gum arabic, the resin of the acacia tree, to build miniature castles and trees, but in Europe, where gum arabic was harder to come by, marzipan was the medium of choice.[89] Those Sicilian nuns weren't the only ones to use it as modelling clay. Leonardo da Vinci expressed grave disappointment each time his patron Ludovico Sforza allowed his courtiers to eat the sculptures and architectural models the artist had created.[90]

In England, marzipan "subtleties" were served between courses, a subtlety being something fine, rare, or cleverly wrought. Subtleties came in the shapes of stags, boars, castles, and, especially, heraldic devices.

In the craft below, I suggest matcha (green tea) powder to color the marzipan. You can make a third color by making a batch of "dark marzipan" using unblanched almonds. Dark marzipan can also be substituted for blanched marzipan in any of the recipes, except the marzipan potatoes (where you want the paler skin of the "potato" to show through the cocoa powder) and for the sun and moon shields. Because almond skins are high in fiber, dark marzipan is healthier than white.

These little shields will look very impressive at the center of your Advent cookie plate. They can, of course, be eaten after you're done showing them off. If the shield template provided is too small to accommodate the cookie cutter "devices" you want to use, you can, of course, make a larger template.

---

89. Mintz, *Sweetness and Power*, 79.

90. Eigeland, "Arabs, Almonds, Sugar, and Toledo."

Craft

MARZIPAN COATS OF ARMS

Tools

Paper

Scissors

One batch homemade marzipan or 1 cup (about 300 grams)
store-bought marzipan

½ teaspoon matcha (Japanese green tea) powder

Powdered sugar for dusting surface

Rose water

Small paintbrush

Plastic soda bottle cap or another small cap

Small cookie cutters (optional)

Trace the shield template (Figure 6f) and cut out. These can be
found in the appendix on page 257.

Figure 6f

To make striped shields, divide your homemade marzipan in two. Shape one into a ball and wrap in plastic. Knead the matcha powder into the second half, adding the matcha a little at a time so you can control how dark you want it. Shape into a ball and wrap up until ready to use. You now have one ball of plain marzipan and one of green. Always keep the portion you are not working with wrapped to keep it moist.

Dust your surface with powdered sugar and roll out the plain marzipan. Use a sharp knife to cut around the template to make a few shields.

Roll out and cut a shield from the green marzipan. Gently lay it over one of the plain shields (you don't want them to stick) and cut both in half lengthwise then diagonally as shown in Figure 6g.

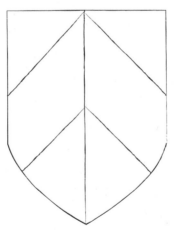

Figure 6g

Disassemble and reassemble the shields, mixing up the colors. Paint each edge with rose water to make them stick when you gently press them together. Do the same with the rest of the dough (Figure 6h).

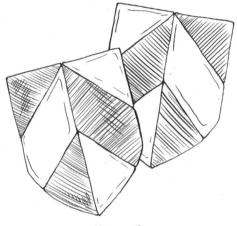

Figure 6h

To make a shield with a Christmassy heraldic device, cut the shield out of one color and the device out of another with a cookie cutter, gluing it on with rose water. Let all shields dry for a few hours.

To make sun and moon shields, you need only plain marzipan.

Divide the dough in two and cut some plain shields out as before. Using a butter knife (not a sharp knife), score each shield as shown (Figure 6i). Don't cut all the way through. Set your shields aside while you make the devices.

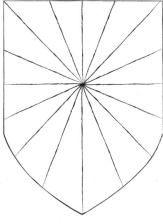

Figure 6i

Press your plastic cap into the marzipan to cut out round suns and crescent moons. Use the point of a chopstick and the tip of a knife to give them eyes, nose, and mouth. Glue each sun and moon onto the center of a shield with rose water and toast them as for Königsberger marzipan (Figures 6j and 6k). The scored lines will be paler, giving your celestial bodies a radiant appearance.

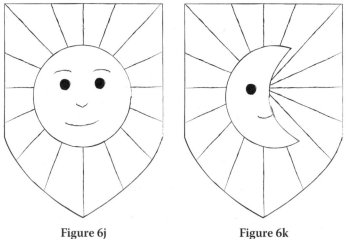

Figure 6j   **Figure 6k**

Linzer Torte

The latticework Linzer Torte that Austrians eat at Christmas (and which we do, too, ever since my mother found a recipe in a magazine) was first baked by Benedictine nuns in the Austrian city of Linz in the late 1600s. My mother never ate Linzer Torte as a child, but she remembers eating the downsized *Linzertörtchen,* "little Linzer tarts" (sometimes called *Linzer augen,* "Linzer eyes"), at Lübeck's Christmas market where a ring of piped marzipan took the place of the dough lattice.

LINZER TARTLETS

Ingredients for the Dough
½ cup (113 grams) plus 2 tablespoons butter
1 cup (198 grams) sugar
1 egg
Zest of one small lemon
1 teaspoon cinnamon
⅛ teaspoon cloves
2 cups (240 grams) flour
1¼ cups (179 cups) roasted, skinned, ground hazelnuts

For the Filling
Half a 12-ounce (340-gram) jar red currant or seedless raspberry jam

For the Piping
1 egg white
⅓ cup (66 grams) sugar
¼ teaspoon almond extract

1 cup (84 grams) ground, blanched almonds (blanched
    almonds look more traditional, but I like to use
    unblanched)

To make the dough, cream the butter and sugar. Add the eggs,
lemon zest, cinnamon, and cloves. Mix well.

Stir in the flour and hazelnuts. Shape dough into a ball and
roll it out on floured surface to ¼-inch thickness. Cut into circles with a small juice glass. Put the circles on a cookie sheet
and spread each with jam all the way to the edge.

To make the piping, beat the egg white to stiff peaks. Stir
in the almonds, almond extract, and sugar. Spoon the sticky
mess into a piping bag and, using a fluted tip, pipe around the
edge of each cookie. If the fluting isn't holding its shape, let the
mixture dry for half an hour and try again.

Bake the cookies at 350 F (177 C) for twenty minutes or
until the piping is a very light golden brown. Makes about
thirty-six.

Christmas Corn

Early advertisements for Goelitz Candy Corn show Santa Claus dropping a box of the striped, corn-shaped sweets down the chimney. The business of molding and coloring marzipan into fun, festive shapes was brought to North America by German immigrants, but the price of almonds placed marzipan out of reach for most Americans, especially in the rural Midwest. Marzipan's place was soon taken by buttercream, sometimes called mellocreme, a much cheaper, moldable mixture of melted sugar and corn syrup.[91]

Setting up shop in Cincinnati, Ohio, in the late nineteenth century, Adolph Goelitz designed his buttercreams to look like the dried corn kernels farm children fed to their chickens. He filled the tiny molds in three layers to create horizontal stripes of white, orange, and yellow.[92] But how did this "Universal Christmas Confection," as candy corns were advertised, become the universal Halloween candy? It may simply have been a matter of getting them on store shelves earlier and earlier in the season so that, by the 1930s, when Mischief Night pranks were being superseded by the friendlier practice of trick-or-treating, candy corns were the natural choice for appeasing the neighborhood spooks.

But what about those unnatural-looking horizontal stripes? If you ask me, the Goelitzes had always had their eyes

---

91. *Mello* for *mallow*, a wetland relative of the hollyhock, whose milky roots Early American settlers used to make the first marshmallows.

92. Geschenke 2015, "The Devil's Earwax: A Cincinnati Candy Invented for Christmas, Not Halloween," November 2, 2021, https://dannwoellertthefoodetymologist.wordpress.com/2021/11/02/the-devils-earwax-a-cincinnati-german-candy-invented-for-christmas-not-halloween/.

on Halloween. Adolph's father, Gustav, had emigrated from Germany's Harz Mountains, a region famous for its gaily dressed peasant witches who fly around in kerchiefs, clogs, and horizontally striped stockings.[93]

93. Christina Bearden-White, "Gustav Goelitz," Immigrant Entrepreneurship, last updated August 22, 2018, https://www.immigrantentrepreneurship.org/entries/gustav-goelitz/.

Chapter Seven
All Wrapped Up

E gypt is home to one of the earliest Christian sects, the Coptic Church, and there are shades of the Black Land in European Christmas observances—statues of the goddess Isis holding her breast out to the infant Horus foreshadowing sculptures of the Virgin Mary suckling the baby Jesus. A shepherd's crook like the one carried by the Dutch St. Nicholas appears in the golden fist of Tutankhamun on the lid of his outermost coffin, and the New Kingdom baking tradition lives on in the *qurban*, the round loaf that Coptic Christians take home with them after mass on Christmas Day (January 7). Decorated with a cross inside a circle of twelve dots, the *qurban*, "offering," represents Jesus and his twelve apostles.[94] The Holy Nativity Fast, which precedes the Coptic celebration of Christmas on January 7, may have been the foundation for the medieval European Advent when meat, cheese, eggs, and dairy were forbidden.

Switching from butter to freshly pressed olive oil for the duration of St. Martin's Lent was no hardship for those Christians living in warmer climates, but the folk up north had

---

94. Nadia Osman, "What's Different about Coptic Christmas?" Middle East Eye, January 7, 2020, https://www.middleeasteye.net/discover/what-different-about -coptic-christmas.

only two choices: buy expensive, often rancid, imported olive oil from Italy, or use their own homegrown rapeseed oil.[95] In May, the landscape of Germany's northernmost province, Schleswig-Holstein, lights up with fields of bright yellow rape flowers, known in the United States as "canola," the source of the neutral-tasting oil many of us bake with today. But this variety of rapeseed has only existed since the 1960s. Back in the fourteenth century, rapeseed oil was good only for burning in lamps.

To remedy the situation, Ernest, Elector of Saxony (1441–1486) petitioned a total of five popes over a period of forty years—i.e., most of his short life—for the right to use butter during Advent.[96] When permission was finally granted a few years after Ernest's death, it came with a price: the donation of funds to rebuild fire-damaged Freiburg Cathedral. It wasn't until 1527, when the state of Saxony became Protestant and the pope's rules no longer applied, that Saxony's signature Christmas cake, Stollen, came into its own.[97]

The quintessential Stollen is the Dresdner Christstollen, which, with its heavy dusting of powdered sugar, is supposed to resemble the Baby Jesus in his snow-white swaddling clothes. It was to Egypt that the Holy Family fled to escape King Herod's Slaughter of the Holy Innocents on December 28, and though mummification during the Graeco-Roman period was no longer the high art it had been in the days of

---

95. Metzger, *Culinaria Germany*, 38.

96. An Elector was a prince who was allowed to cast a vote in the election of the Holy Roman Emperor.

97. Bäckerei Gnauck, "The History of the Christ Stollen from Dresden," accessed January 24, 2023, ." https://www.stollen-online.de/dresdnerstollen/geschichte-eng.htm.

the pharaohs, the Egyptians were still wizards when it came to wrapping humans, cats, and other creatures in linen bands. I imagine Mary must have picked up some neat swaddling tricks while she was there.

The name *Stollen*, however, has nothing to do with babies, swaddled or otherwise. A *Stollen* can be a supporting post or stud, like the log that was used to hold up the ceiling of a mining gallery, or the tunnel itself.[98] Miners have been working the depths of Saxony's Erzbegirbe or "ore mountains" since 2500 BCE, first for tin then silver then cobalt, a potentially poisonous element that is used to paint the blue designs on the fine porcelain cake plates off which slices of Stollen are still eaten today.

For thousands of years, the mineral cobalt's namesake, the *Kobold*, worked alongside the Saxon miners. On the rare occasions when the Kobold allowed himself to be seen, he appeared as a hunched little man, but most of the time he was invisible, communicating with the miners by knocking on the rock. If you treated the Kobold with respect, he would lead you to the best veins and warn you of danger. If you were rude to him, he might kick aside one of those Stollen and cause a cave-in.

Here in America, my paternal grandmother, who grew up not far from the city of Dresden, served her Stollen on red willow–patterned plates, but when it came to the baking of the Stollen, she stuck to tradition. Because she couldn't get them

---

98. View the official website of the Dresdner Stollen Verband in English and you'll see reference to a "Stud girl." This is the Dresdner Stollenmädchen who is elected each year to represent the guild. (She has nothing to do with procreation.) Dresdner Stollen Verband e.V., "Dresdner Christstollen," accessed February 18, 2022, https://www.dresdnerstollen.com/de/.

in New Jersey, she asked her family back in East Germany to send her a tiny packet of bitter almonds each year. Yes, bitter almonds contain deadly cyanide, but my grandmother never used enough of them to kill anyone. She made her Stollen early in the season and stored it in an unheated attic bedroom, waiting until very close to Christmas before she started doling it out, half slice by half slice, with afternoon coffee.

Author Stephen Mack got his first taste of Stollen when the German translator of a book he'd written about World War II's Navajo code talkers stopped by his Tucson, Arizona, home one December, bearing the gift of an authentic Dresdner Christstollen. Steve is still on the fence when it comes to Stollen: "The first bite: not sure I liked it. The second: not bad. Third: it was absolutely exquisite." He told me he goes through the same three stages each time he eats a slice. I suspect it's the unfamiliar-to-the-American-palate cardamom that gives him pause.

Stollen comes in two forms: slit down the middle or folded over. My grandmother's Stollen, which she folded over, was indeed about the size of a newborn Baby Jesus. The recipe below makes a smaller one. If you decide you like it, you can double the recipe next time, but better to try a little one first.

As desserts go, Stollen is not very sweet, which is probably why our family's has migrated from Advent coffee to Christmas morning breakfast. If you want to make your Stollen a little sweeter, it's perfectly acceptable to insert a log of homemade marzipan before folding the dough over and putting it in the oven.

Genuine Dresdner Christstollen contains candied bitter orange and citron peel. If you can get them, use them. If not, go with your own homemade candied orange and lemon peel.

Note: Real Stollen shouldn't have any candied cherries in it. If it does, it's not Stollen; it's just Christmas fruit bread.

CHRISTSTOLLEN

Ingredients

½ cup (975 grams) golden raisins (sultanas)

½ cup (74 grams) black raisins

½ cup (118 milliliters) rum

½ cup (113 grams) butter, plus another tablespoon for "icing"

½ cup (118 milliliters) whole milk

One .25-ounce packet (7 grams) active dry yeast

⅓ cup (966 grams) sugar plus another tablespoon for sprinkling

2 cups (240 grams) flour, plus about ¼ cup (30 grams) for kneading

¼ teaspoon nutmeg

¼ teaspoon cardamom

⅛ teaspoon mace

½ cup (42 grams) blanched, ground almonds

2 teaspoons almond extract

1 tablespoon candied citron or lemon peel, chopped

1 tablespoon candied orange peel, chopped

1 teaspoon lemon zest

¼ cup powdered sugar

Soak all the raisins in the rum for at least twenty-four hours.

In a small pot, heat the butter and milk just until the butter is melted.

In a large bowl, mix the yeast, 1 tablespoon of the flour, 1 tablespoon of the sugar, and 2 tablespoons of hot water. Set aside for five minutes. If bubbles form, you know your yeast is alive and well.

Add the rest of the flour a little at a time, alternating with the buttermilk mixture. Turn the dough onto a floured surface and knead in the extra ¼ cup of flour along with the spices, ground almonds, almond extract, candied peels, and lemon zest. Knead the dough for about ten minutes before adding a tablespoon of the rum from the soaking raisins.

Drain the raisins well and work them in, too.

Shape the dough into a ball, cover with a dish towel, and let rise in a warm place for an hour.

Punch the dough down and roll into a stout pillar. Cover and let rest for ten minutes.

Transfer your Stollen to a cookie sheet. With a sharp knife, make a cut down the middle, lengthwise, about an inch deep. This is the "cut" style of Stollen. If you are making a marzipan Stollen, you must use the "wrap" style, placing the marzipan log on top of the pillar, lengthwise, and folding the dough over it. Don't worry about the fold showing; it's supposed to.

Put your Stollen in the oven and turn the dial to 350 F (177 C). German recipes go into a cold oven, so no preheating! Bake for thirty-five to forty minutes or until golden. (The dough inside the slit will be a little paler.)

Transfer the hot Stollen to a wooden board and remove any burnt raisins from the top. Brush the Stollen with the tablespoon of butter, immediately sprinkling the tablespoon of sugar over it. Let cool for five minutes and sift with the powdered sugar, tilting the board to make sure you get the sides, too.

Let your Stollen cool completely before wrapping it in plastic, then in foil. Store it in a cool place for at least a few days before serving.

Seax and *Striezel*

The Saxons were named for the short sword or *seax* the Saxon warrior carried. The Saxons were first mentioned by the Greek geographer Ptolemy around 150 BCE at which time they were living on the North Sea. The great millings-around of populations known as the Migration Period tossed some of the Saxons up on the east coast of Britain, along with the Angles, and drove others into what is now the province of Saxony in eastern Germany.

The only knives Saxons carry nowadays are Stollen knives. Augustus II, known as the Strong, Elector of Saxony and King of Poland, was all about pomp. In 1730, he commissioned the forging of a giant knife to cut the giant Stollen, which was the centerpiece of Dresden's *Striezelmarkt*, *Striezel* being another name for Stollen that was still in use when the market was founded in 1434.[99] How a knife so heavy that it needed two men to carry it should go missing is a mystery to me, but it's gone. The silver-plated Grand Dresden Stollen Knife that's trotted out nowadays is a less ornate replica.

Steel Stollen knives, which look more like scimitars than short swords, are used to chop the candied bitter orange and citron peel that go into genuine Dresdner Christstollen, while silver ones are used to slice and serve the finished product.

My Saxon grandmother died when I was five, taking her traditional Dresdner Stollen recipe, which she never wrote

99. Metzger, *Culinaria Germany*, 38.

down, with her. It was then that my mother, a lover of short-cuts with no experience in making yeast doughs, started making the Baking Powder Stollen in Dr. Oetker's *Backen macht Freude* (The Joy of Baking), adapting it over the years to her own taste and her own American kitchen.

BAKING POWDER STOLLEN

Ingredients

4 cups (480 grams) flour

4 teaspoons baking powder

½ cup (42 grams) blanched, ground almonds

1 cup (198 grams) sugar

¼ teaspoon cardamom

¼ teaspoon mace

¾ cup (1½ sticks) cold butter, plus 1 tablespoon for "icing"

2 eggs, beaten

2 teaspoons almond extract

1 teaspoon vanilla extract

1 teaspoon rum extract

1 cup (227 grams) *Quark,*[100] farmer's, or Neufchatel cheese

2 tablespoons lemon zest

2 tablespoons candied citron or lemon peel

½ cup (75 grams) Zante currants

½ cup (75 grams) black raisins

½ cup (75 grams) golden raisins (sultanas)

½ cup (56 grams) powdered sugar for dusting

---

100. A fresh German cheese that you can sometimes find in the grocery store near the Greek yogurt and Icelandic *skyr*.

In a large bowl, mix half the flour with the baking powder, almonds, sugar, and spices. Cut in the cold butter. Turn everything out onto the kitchen table, make a well in the center, and add the eggs and extracts, working them in with your hands. Work in the *Quark*, the rest of the flour, zest, peel, currants, raisins, and golden raisins.

When you've managed to make a smooth (except for the fruits) dough, put it on a greased or parchment-lined cookie sheet and pat it into a flat oval. Fold the oval over, not quite in half, so that the edge is not quite in the middle (Figure 7a).

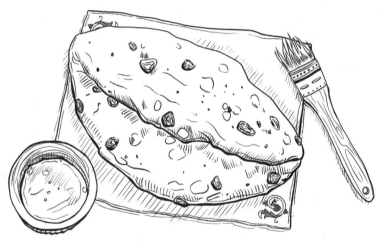

Figure 7a

Bake at 325 F (165 C) for seventy-five minutes or until lightly browned.

Brush your Stollen with butter immediately and dust it with powdered sugar.

Figure 7b

Figure 7c

When it's completely cool, wrap it in plastic then in foil and store it in a cool place, but not on a lower shelf in a garage frequented by a hungry German shepherd. This has happened.

Stollen Paper Seal

If you've ever had a German Advent calendar, you've probably seen tribes of gnomes, angels, and rosy-cheeked children rushing about with Stollen wrapped in white paper and bound with red ribbons held in place with red wax seals. This is the old-fashioned way to wrap a Stollen. If you don't have any sealing wax, you can still wrap yours in white paper and tie it with red ribbon. You can even apply a paper seal. The official seal of the Dresdner Stollen Protective Association, featuring Augustus the Strong on a rearing horse, can only be applied to authentic Dresdner Stollen. (I wouldn't be surprised if Rekhmire had some similar way of marking his tiger nut cakes.) But you can make your own seal to apply to your own Stollen or any other of your baked goods.

PAPER SEAL

Tools and Materials
White paper
Gold paint
Scissors
Glue
Black pen

Draw a circle at least two inches in diameter on the white paper. Cut out and paint one side gold. Cut another circle about ⅜ of an inch smaller. Fold the first circle into quarters, plain side out, and cut points as shown (Figure 7d). Unfold.

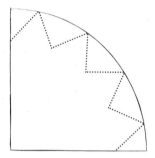

Figure 7d

Draw your personal device inside the second circle and glue it over the first circle, gold side up (Figure 7e).

Figure 7e

Sorbian Tradition

Despite violent incursions by the missionizing Order of Teutonic Knights, not to mention oppression by the Nazis before and during World War II, Saxony's Slavic-speaking Sorbs (historically known as Wends) managed to survive with their culture and language intact, both of which they maintain in the region of Upper Lusatia today. The Christmas market in the Lusatian town of Hoyerswerda (Sorbian Wojerecy) is called the Teschen-markt in honor of Imperial Princess Ursula Katharina von Teschen (1680–1743). Following her divorce from a Polish prince, Ursula Katharina became Augustus the Strong's mistress.

Cast off by the fickle Augustus five years later, Ursula Katharina retreated to the rural town of Hoyerswerda, home of the boy wizard Krabat, hero of Otfried Preußler's 1971 children's novel of the same name. Once she'd dried her tears, Ursula Katharina devoted herself to turning the little farming town into a center of industry. The princess still shows up each year (plagues notwithstanding) to open the Teschen-markt and to cut Hoyerswerda's own giant Stollen. She is accompanied by a colorful cast of characters in eighteenth-century court dress and by the *Weihnachtsmann*, the German Santa Claus.[101]

In his bright red coat and hood, the Weihnachtsmann clearly belongs to Teutonic tradition, but if you keep your eyes peeled, you might catch a glimpse of the enigmatic *Bože dźěćetko*, the Sorbian Christ Child. Despite the name, Bože

---

101. Hoyerswerda.de, "Das war der Weihnachtsmarkt," December 17, 2018, https://www.hoyerswerda.de/2018/12/17/das-war-der-weihnachtsmarkt/.

dźěćetko makes no attempt to look like a boy. Dressed in full peasant skirts topped by a white apron, she carries a bundle of birch twigs and a bell, except when she is using her white lace–gloved hands to stroke the faces of the children hoping to get candy from the basket held by her attendant. Like the Barborka who visits Bohemian children on the eve of St. Barbara's Day (December 4), the Bože dźěćetko covers her face in white lace and speaks not a word.[102]

Sorbs bake the same Stollen and Christmas cookies as their ethnic German neighbors, but on January 25, they bake sweet buns called *sroki* (singular *sroka*, "magpie")—at least, the birds do. These blobby, raisin-eyed bird buns are part of the uniquely Sorbian tradition of the Birds' Wedding. Almost all Germans know the folksong *Die Vogelhochzeit*, "The Birds' Wedding," but only in Lusatia does the name apply to a day of celebration when girls dress up in white pinafores and trailing satin headdresses, boys in top hats and tails, to parade through the snow in a reenactment of the wedding of the rook bridegroom to his magpie bride.[103] The night before the Birds' Wedding, children set empty plates on their windowsills so the birds can leave them gifts. In the old days, this meant a sweet porridge of prunes and millet (think frumenty), but nowadays

---

102. Guido Erbrich, Rafael Ledschbor, Anja Pohontsch, and Mirko Pohontsch, *Wo Krabat das Zaubern lernte: Unterwegs in sorbischen Oberlausitz* (Bautzen, Germany: Domowina-Verlag, 2010), 52–53.

103. Erbrich, et al., *Wo Krabat das Zaubern lernte*, 42. In the German folksong, the groom is a thrush and the bride is a blackbird.

there are candies and both yeast dough sroki and sroki made of meringue.[104]

Why January 25? I'm not sure, but January 25 is also the Feast of the Conversion of St. Paul, who was overtaken by the Holy Ghost on the way to Damascus.[105] The Holy Ghost is often represented as a dove, so maybe the magpies were originally doves? Sroki aren't a Christmas food, but because the Birds' Wedding falls between Christmas Day and Candlemas (February 2), the official last gasp of the season in the medieval calendar, I'm including a recipe here.

Recipe

Sroki

Ingredients

4 tablespoons (56 grams) butter

A little less than 1 cup (236 milliliters) milk

Two .25-ounce packets rapid rise active dry yeast (14 grams)

¼ cup (50 grams) sugar

---

104. Erbrich, et al, *Wo Krabat das Zaubern lernte*, 43; Metger, *Culinaria Germany*, 44; The meringue sroki look so much like marshmallow Peeps that I wondered if the former could have inspired the latter. Alas, according to ancestry.com, Peeps inventor Roscoe E. Rodda was born in Michigan to immigrant parents from Cornwall, England. Before Ukrainian Jewish immigrant Sam Born automated the Peep-making process in 1953, each chick had been formed by hand, using real marshmallow, i. e., the mucilaginous root of the marshmallow plant (*Althea officinalis*). Still, if you want to celebrate the Birds' Wedding and don't want to go to the trouble of baking buns or meringues, Peeps are a suitable alternative. Matt Blitz, "The History of Peeps," Food and Wine, last updated May 24, 2017, https://www.foodandwine.com/news/history-peeps.

105. Martin Schönleben, "Gebackene Vögelchen – 25 Januar Sankt Pauli Bekehrung," January 19, 2013, https://cafeschoenleben.de /gebackene-vogelchen-25-januar-sankt-pauli-bekehrung/.

3½ cups (about 420 grams) flour
2 eggs, beaten
20 whole cloves

For the Icing
1 cup (113 grams) powdered sugar
1½ tablespoons milk
⅛ teaspoon almond or vanilla extract

In a small pot, heat the butter and milk together just until the butter is melted.

In a large bowl, mix the yeast with the sugar and a ¼ cup of the flour. Add to this a ¼ cup of the warm milk/butter mixture, stirring well. Set aside in a warm place for ten minutes. If bubbles form, you'll know your yeast is active.

To the large bowl, add the rest of the milk/butter mixture, more of the flour, and the eggs, stirring well. Add the rest of the flour, kneading the last half cup in by hand on a board or table. Continue to knead ten minutes. Put the dough in a greased bowl, cover with a damp towel, and let rise in a warm place for half an hour.

Punch the dough down and roll it flat on a floured surface. Cut it into about ten pieces, roll each piece into a ball as best as you can, and set the balls on a baking sheet, leaving at least two inches between each ball.

Cover and let rise for half an hour.

Roll each ball into an eight-inch rope with a fat bulb at one end—this will be the magpie's head.[106] Coil each rope so the head is on top. Leave the end of the rope sticking out behind.

106. To see how the proferssionals do it, see Załožba Stiftung, "Sroka k ptačemu – Backen der 'sroka' zur Vogelhochzeit," January 22.2021, https://www.youtube .com/watch?v=Ll3qNLrWD00&t=2s.

This is the tail. Cut the tail in two lengthwise and spread the "tail feathers." Stick the cloves in for eyes (Figure 7f).

Figure 7f

Cover with a damp towel and let rest for ten minutes. The weight of the towel will help them hold their shape.

Bake at 350 F (177 C) for fifteen to twenty minutes or until golden brown. While they're baking, prepare your icing.

Let buns cool about five minutes before spooning the icing over the finished sroki. They taste best when eaten the same day (Figure 7g). (Whole cloves are edible, but they're quite hot, so you might want to remove the eyes before biting into the head.)

Figure 7g

Chapter Eight
The Sunny Side of the Alps

I n the Middle Ages, anything sweet was the province of the apothecaries. In Venice, these "specialists" brewed up batches of Teriaca, a supposedly divine and supremely sticky concoction of gum arabic, opium, cinnamon, pepper, fennel, rose petals, powdered amber, stag testicles, unicorn horn, and viper venom. A cure-all for everything but the plague, Teriaca got its name from the Greek *thérion*, meaning "wild animal," the original *theriaca* being used to treat bites from poisonous animals. (The viper venom was included as "hair of the dog.")

In her classic 1960 book *Venice*, the late travel writer Jan Morris described Teriaca as an oozing, "brown treacly fluid."[107] Could she have known that the Greek word *theriaca* had also come to mean the syrup in which the drugs were mixed, i.e., "treacle"? Each apothecary's Teriaca recipe was a closely guarded secret, but the brewing of the potion took place *al fresco*, in full public view. Sunken circles in the pavement of the *Calle dello Spezier*, "Apothecary Street," and other alleyways still mark the spots where the cauldrons were tended.[108]

107. Morris, *Venice*, 70.

108. "Teriaca – The Divine Potion," accessed May 29, 2022, https://imagesofvenice
.com/teriaca-the-divine-potion/.

No one brews Teriaca anymore—at least, not on a large scale—but torrone, a sticky confection of honey, sugar, egg whites, and whole, roasted nuts, is served as the final course of the Italian Christmas dinner. According to the citizens of Cremona, who have claimed the sweet as their own, torrone was invented in 1441 to celebrate the wedding of Francesco Sforza to Bianca Maria Visconti.[109] But torrone is much older than that.

The ancient Romans were under the impression that their torronelike *nucatem*, the ancestor of our "nougat," was the invention of the Samnites, a hard-to-subdue non-Roman tribe living in what is now the city of Benevento about thirty miles north of Naples.[110] After they came under Roman rule, many Samnites joined the imported cult of Isis, conflating the Egyptian moon goddess with the Greek goddess of witchcraft, Hecate. Because the Beneventanos continued to gather under their sacred walnut tree, conducting their pagan rituals well into Christian times, Benevento became known as a city of witches.[111] Torrone is probably more directly descended from *turun*, a sweet of the Arab world, but in the Italian sphere, torrone, Christmas, and witches keep coming together.

109. Piras, *Culinaria Italy*, 108.

110. Massimo Lanari, "The History of Torrone, an Italian Christmas Dessert," November 5, 2020, https://www.lacucinaitaliana.com/italian-food/italian-dishes/the-history-of-torrone-an-italian-christmas-dessert; Pompeii was also a former Samnite territory.

111. Caserta Royal Palace and Park, Italy, "The Benevento Witches," accessed January 24, 2023, https://visitworldheritage.com/en/eu/the-benevento-witches/6453590a-ff50-4a3a-8fe8-0a9a797b7b4e.

The Story of Young Befana

Retired librarian Anne de Furia was the only Italian at the Quaker school she attended in Pennsylvania in the 1960s, which was probably why her teacher picked her to play the role of the Italian Epiphany witch, Befana. Anne's father's family had come from a village in the Apennine Mountains near Naples, but Anne had never heard of "la Befana" before her second-grade class started exchanging letters with children in the north Italian town of Rimini.

Befana gets her name from *Epiphania*, the day the Three Kings arrived in Bethlehem to present gifts of gold, frankincense, and myrrh to the Baby Jesus. The kings, or magi, had invited Befana to come with them, but the old woman decided that sweeping her kitchen floor was more important. Changing her mind, she set out after the kings, carrying her broom with her, but they'd already disappeared over the horizon.

Befana has been looking for the Baby Jesus ever since, flying over Italy on her broomstick and dumping treats down the chimneys of houses where children live. Good children wake up on the morning of January 6 to find toys, chocolates, and maybe some star-shaped pefanino cookies in their stockings. Not-quite-so-good children find onions, garlic, and *Carbone dolce della Befana*, chunks of very realistic-looking "sweet coal" made of egg whites, sugar, and black food coloring, which can be bought at the Befana Market in Rome's Piazza Navona.

On the big day, Anne put on a long skirt, apron, blouse, and kerchief. Not knowing anything about sweet coal or pefanino cookies, she filled a basket with individually wrapped Ferraro torrone she'd found in the sideboard at home. "I felt very important," she says of her performance as the torrone-toting witch.

Anne didn't run into Befana again until she became a librarian and found her old friend in the pages of Tomie DePaola's 1980 picture book *The Legend of Old Befana.* DePaola's witch is very plainly dressed, but I have decorated mine's shawl and headscarf with the patterns he painted on the borders of the title page.

Paper Befana on a Broomstick

Tools and Materials

1 8½" by 11" sheet plain white paper

Scissors

Extra-long round toothpick or shish kebab skewer, cut down
    to about 4 inches

Colored pencils or markers

Glue

Loop of gold or silver cord

Cut a 4½-inch square from your sheet of printer paper. (This will be Befana.)

Cut a 2-inch square of paper. (This will be the broom.)

First make the broom: Cut ⅔ of the paper square in a fringe (Figure 8a). Roll the paper tightly around one end of the broomstick, fringe inward (Figure 8b).

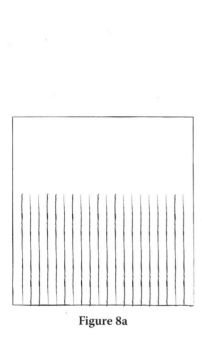

Figure 8a   **Figure 8b**

Glue the end of the paper to secure it. Pull the "bristles" down and wind a thin strip of paper around them (Figure 8c). Glue the end of the strip to secure it.

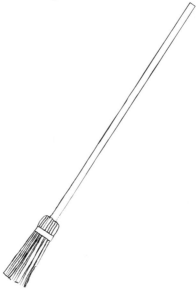

Figure 8c

To make Befana: Crease the 4½-inch square of paper as shown (Figure 8d).

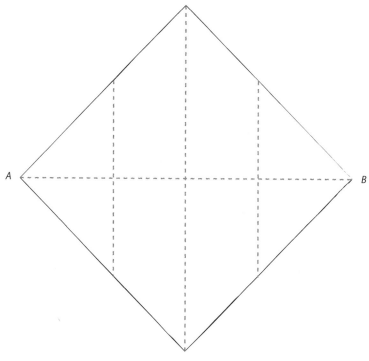

Figure 8d

Fold points A and B in so that they overlap slightly at the center line (Figure 8e).

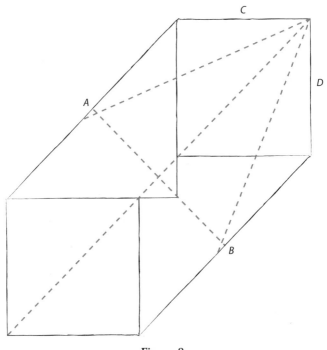

Figure 8e

Fold edges C and D in to the center line (Figure 8f).

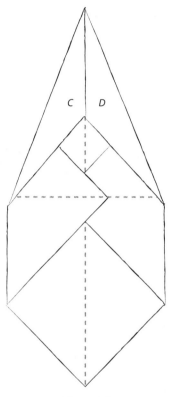

Figure 8f

Fold the model in half and cut to make a nose. Fold point E down along the dotted line in Figure 8g. Fold point F up along the other dotted line in Figure 8g. Unfold both and fold the other way, creasing well (Figure 8g).

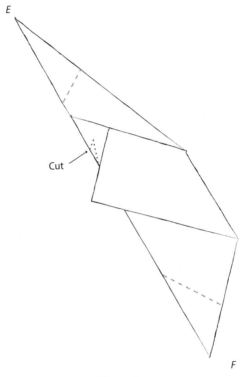

Figure 8g

Using that dotted line that you have now folded both ways, fold point E down inside Befana's kerchief. Cut along Befana's center line from "feet" to "hands" and fold point(s) F back on either side along the crease you made (Figure 8h).

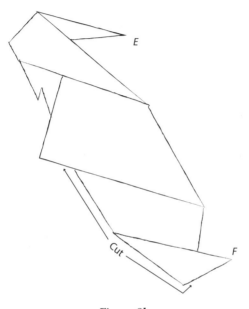

Figure 8h

Decorate Befana's shawl and kerchief and cut the fringe on her shawl. Glue your loop of cord inside her kerchief. Insert her broom and glue in place (Figure 8i).

Figure 8i

Strong Bread

The tricky torrone is best made by the apothecaries' heirs, the confectioners, but Sienese *panforte*, coming in halfway between candy and cake, is fairly easy to make at home. Like the Venetian Teriaca brewers, Siena's medieval apothecaries kept their recipes for *panpepato*, a "peppered bread" of honey, sugar, dried fruits, nuts, and spices, under lock and key. Siena's landowning monasteries were accustomed to receiving pan-pepato as a tax, but sometime in the twelfth century, the nuns started baking their own version, which they called *panforte*, "strong bread." There was nothing new, of course, about putting honey, nuts, and fruits together. What was new was the steady stream of spices and sugar now flowing out of Venice. The next great panforte innovation, and the best as far as I'm concerned, was the addition of cocoa powder in the 1800s.

The old panpepato tax was due on February 7, but the new panforte soon rose to prominence as a Christmas dessert.[112] You will hear it referred to as the oldest Christmas "cake," but its consistency is a lot more like torrone than Lebkuchen. In fact, a panforte is roughly the consistency and shape of an oversized hockey puck, qualities that have not been lost on the Sienese, who wrap it in brown paper, wind it four times around with string, and pitch it across a long table. The pitching takes place in the piazza where a long wooden table is set up just for this purpose. The object of the game? To slide the

---

112. Un po' di pepe, "Panforte di Siena," December 12, 2020, https://unpodipepe
.ca/2020/12/12/panforte-di-siena/.

mummified panforte as far down the table as one can without it falling off the edge.[113]

Panforte

Note: These days, most panforte do not contain figs, but the old panpepato did. Because I like figs, I have put them back in.

Ingredients
½ cup (71 grams) roasted, skinned hazelnuts

½ cup (71 grams) blanched almonds

¼ cup (35 grams) pine nuts

½ cup (75 grams) chopped, dried figs

⅓ cup (57 grams) candied orange peel, chopped somewhat fine

⅓ cup (57 grams) candied lemon peel, chopped somewhat fine

½ cup (60 grams) flour

¼ cup (21 grams) unsweetened cocoa

1 teaspoon cinnamon

⅓ cup (57 grams) dark chocolate, chopped

1 teaspoon ginger

1 teaspoon black pepper

½ cup (100 grams) sugar

¼ cup (85 grams) honey

113. Rick Steves and Valerie Griffith, *Rick Steves' European Christmas* (Emeryville, California: Avalon Travel Publishing, 2005), 199.

Generous dash sweet red wine (optional—I like to use the
   wine in which I've soaked the currants for my peverini)
Powdered sugar for dusting

Line an 8-inch cake pan or springform with baking parchment.

Chop the hazelnuts and almonds coarsely. (Leave the pine nuts whole.)

In a large bowl, mix the flour with the cocoa, spices, and chocolate. Add the nuts, figs, and peel. Set aside.

In a small pot, heat the sugar and honey on low heat, stirring until the sugar is dissolved. When the entire surface is covered in large bubbles, turn the heat off and pour the mixture immediately into the bowl with the other ingredients. Add the wine and mix well with a strong wooden spoon. The dough will be stiff, sticky, and difficult. Keep turning and scraping until you get everything in.

Turn the dough into the pan and press with the back of a wet spoon until it meets the edge. (Panforte is thin.)

Bake at 300 F (150 C) for fifty minutes.

Lift your panforte out of the pan, parchment and all, and let it cool completely. When cool, wrap it tightly in plastic wrap for at least a day before dusting with powdered sugar and cutting into thin wedges to serve with coffee.

Star-Crossed Cake

The name *Nadalin* comes from *Natale*, "Christmas." As its name suggests, this star-shaped cake has always been baked for Christmas. It was invented in the mid-thirteenth century in the kitchens of the Della Scala family, who ruled Verona from 1262 to 1387.[114] One of the biggest problems facing the Della Scalas was the ongoing feuding among Veronese families, the most famous combatants being the members of the Montecchi and Cappelleti families. The situation was bad enough that Italian poet Dante (1265–1321) complained of their "open strife" in his *Divine Comedy*.[115] People were still talking about them in 1550 when Franciscan friar Matteo Bandello wrote down the story of a young Montecchi man who fell for a Cappelletti girl, with tragic results.[116]

When Shakespeare got wind of the story, he anglicized their names to Montague and Capulet. Friar Matteo wasn't just a chronicler but a writer of original stories, so the actual events were probably less dramatic than those in *Romeo and Juliet*. I like to think that the real Romeo and Giulietta might have gotten a happy ending, though the ongoing power struggle between the popes and the Holy Roman Emperors, which may have been at the heart of the feud, makes this unlikely.[117] Either way, the star-crossed lovers would both have enjoyed this sweet, lightly leavened cake at Christmastime as children. Blood may have been running in Verona's streets, but the baking of Nadalin was one thing the Veronese could agree on.

---

114. Cristina Pozza, "Traditional Veronese Christmas Cakes," Guide Verona-Italy, December 24, 2021, http://www.guideverona.net/traditional-veronese-christmas-cakes/.

115. John Callas, "Montecchi and Capalletti," Shakespeare Electronic Conference, Volume 4, Number 408, July 2, 1993, https://shaksper.net/archive/1993/89-july/1318-montecchi-and-cappelletti.

116. Callas, "Montecchi and Capalletti."

117. Dan, "Dante and Shakespeare: A Tale of Montagues and Capulets," November 17, 2013, https://secretsofinferno.wordpress.com/2013/11/17/dante-and-shakespeare-a-tale-of-montagues-and-capulets/.

Unlike the later Milanese panettone with its handful of raisins and candied peels, the body of the Nadalin contains only a little lemon zest. The party, so to speak, is on top: a sugary crust of egg, almonds, pine nuts, and marsala wine. Some Nadalin have five points, others eight. Whether baked in a special pan or shaped by hand, it is not a tall star, just a chubby one. If you don't have a star-shaped Nadalin pan, you can bake yours in an eight-inch springform.

NADALIN

Ingredients for the Cake
¾ cups (177 milliliters) milk
1 tablespoon honey
¼ cup (56 grams) butter
½ cup (100 grams) sugar
1 .25-ounce package (7 grams) rapid rise yeast
2¾ cups (330 grams) flour plus a little more for kneading
1 egg, beaten
Zest of one small lemon
1 tablespoon rum extract

For the Topping
⅛ cup (19 milliliters) marsala or other sweet red wine
1 egg yolk
¼ cup (28 grams) slivered almonds
¼ cup (35 grams) pine nuts
¼ cup (50 grams) sugar

In a small pot, heat the milk, honey, and butter until the butter melts. Don't let it boil.

In a large bowl, mix the sugar, yeast, and ½ cup of the flour. Stir the warm milk mixture into the flour mixture. Stir in the egg along with the rum extract. Add another ½ cup of the flour and mix well. Gradually add the rest of the flour.

Turn the dough onto a floured surface and knead for ten minutes. Shape into a ball, put in a greased bowl, and cover. Let the dough rise in a warm place for thirty minutes.

Grease your springform or star-shaped mold.

Punch the dough down. Shape it into a ball and place it in the mold or pan.

Let rise another thirty minutes.

Pat the almonds and pine nuts gently into the top of the risen dough. Stir the egg yolk and wine together and spoon it over the nuts. Use a pastry brush to spread it around. Sprinkle sugar over all.

Bake at 350 F (177 C) for thirty-five to forty minutes.

Let your Nadalin cool before turning it carefully out of the pan and serving it nuts side up.

Bread of Gold

The tall, star-shaped pandoro, which is richer than the more widely imported panettone, is a descendant of Nadalin, whose nutty topping has been replaced by a snowy dusting of vanilla-flavored powdered sugar. Though it originated in Verona, pandoro is the unofficial Christmas cake of Venice.

Pandoro means "bread of gold," after the egg yolks that give it its golden color. It is also said that the fabulously rich Venetians used to dust it with real gold. One might be surprised to learn that a cake favored by the people who kept Europe's spice cabinets stocked throughout the Middle Ages contains no spices whatsoever, but for much of the Middle Ages, eggs, cream, and butter were just as expensive as pepper and ginger. It's also possible that, in a city awash with spices, to make a Christmas cake without any spice at all was the ultimate refinement.

Making pandoro is a time-consuming affair, but there's plenty of time to drink tea and eat cookies between risings. Even if you're not ready to make pandoro yet, you should get your vanilla bean into the powdered sugar as soon as possible. If you don't have a star-shaped pandoro pan, you can bake yours in a Bundt form or an eight-inch springform. If using a springform, follow the instructions at the end of the recipe to make a powdered sugar star on top of your cake.

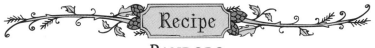

Recipe

PANDORO

Ingredients

1½ .25-ounce packets (a little more than 10 grams) rapid rise yeast

1 cup (120 grams) bread flour plus another ⅓ cup (40 grams) for dusting table and hands

⅓ cup (66 grams) sugar

1 egg, beaten, plus 2 egg yolks

5 tablespoons butter (1½ tablespoons softened, 3½ tablespoons cold)

Zest of 1 lemon

1 teaspoon vanilla extract

¼ cup (59 milliliters) heavy cream

⅛ cup (15 grams) powdered sugar in which a vanilla bean has been hanging around

In a large bowl, mix the yeast with a handful of the bread flour and 1 tablespoon of the sugar. Add 1 tablespoon of hot tap water and the egg yolk. Stir well to make a wet dough. Cover the bowl with a dish towel and let rise in a warm place forty-five minutes. If it looks a little foamy when you uncover it, it means your yeast is active and you can proceed.

Sift ½ cup (60 grams) of the flour over the dough in the bowl. Sprinkle in 2 tablespoons of the sugar. Stir the sugar into the dough along with the other yolk and the 1½ tablespoons of softened butter. Use your hands to work the dough into a smooth ball. Let rise again in a warm place for another forty-five minutes.

Sift the rest of the cup of flour into the dough in the bowl. Add the rest of the sugar and the beaten egg. The dough will be sticky.

Turn the dough onto a heavily floured surface and knead it for ten minutes. If needed, you can add more flour to prevent the dough from sticking to your surface. Put the dough back in the bowl, cover, and let rise another forty-five minutes.

Push your fist into the dough to make a well. Put the lemon zest and vanilla extract in the well along with a little of the heavy cream. Work the ingredients in with your hands, adding the rest of the cream a little at a time. Don't cry; the dough will eventually take it all up. You can even pull and fold the dough in the air so you don't have to worry about it sticking in the bowl or to the board. When you've finally achieved a smooth dough, form it into a ball, replace it in the bowl, cover, and refrigerate overnight.

Roll the dough into a rectangle on your floured surface. Cover it with the cold butter, cut into bits. Fold the dough into thirds over the butter and roll out again. Cover it with a dish towel and let rest fifteen minutes.

Grease your pandoro pan, Bundt pan, or springform.

Fold and roll out the dough three more times.

Shape the dough into a ball. If you are using a pandoro pan, simply place it in the pan. If you are using a springform, place it in the middle. If a Bundt pan, roll it gently into a log first. Cover the pan with a dish towel and let rise one hour.

Preheat the oven to 350 F (177 C). Bake your pandoro fifteen minutes or until it's golden on top.

Turn it out of the pan, let cool, and sift with vanilla powdered sugar. If using a springform, make your stencil before sifting the powdered sugar over your pandoro.

To make a stencil, follow the directions for making the star-shaped cookie tray in chapter 6, using the inside of the springform ring to make your circle.[118] Instead of the star, which you can still make into a cookie tray or—why not?—hang in the window, you're going to use the triangles you have cut away.

Place the eight triangles around the edge of your pandoro and sift the powdered sugar over the exposed cake. Remove the triangles carefully to reveal your eight-pointed powdered sugar star.

Water Witches

When the great Venetian lover Giacomo Casanova (1725–1798) was a child, a beautiful woman climbed down his chimney in the middle of the night and cured him of his chronic

---

118. I've had limited success making mini pandoro and Nadalin in star-shaped cookie trays (see chapter 6) made of baking parchment. If you try this, place the tray in a cake pan and fill the pan with sand before you put the dough in the tray. The sand will help the tray hold its shape.

nosebleeds. The visitation had been predicted by an old folk healer his grandmother had taken him to see on the island of Murano the day before. Because the old woman had been attended by numerous black cats, little Giacomo had been in no doubt that she was a witch, nor should he have been; Venice has always been a city of witches.[119]

Murano's cat lady was just one of a long line of Venetian folk healers who turned beeswax, communion wafers, beans, and other items from their kitchen gardens into witchety tools called *stregamenti*. This was all well and good when the cures worked, but when Dionora Buranelle treated a little boy, unsuccessfully, with wine and biscuits (possibly the spicy Venetian *bicciolani*) from the local convent, she was accused of witchcraft.[120]

The witches who take part in Venice's annual Epiphany Witches' Regatta can't work any magic, but they make up a coven like no other. To participate in the regatta, you must be fifty or older and a member of the Canottieri Bucintoro, Venice's oldest rowing club.[121] You must dress as a witch and row your own *mascareta*, a small, flat-bottomed, single-oared boat that has none of the gondola's grace. Did I mention that you must also be a man?

The Regatta de le Befane dates only to 1978, but it's already a hallowed Venetian tradition. Every year on January 6, the middle-aged, mustachioed contestants gather at San Tomá in

119. Morris, *Venice*, 69.

120. Jennifer Palma, "The Witches of Venice," University of Miami, 2017, accessed January 29, 2025, https://news.miami.edu/stories/2017/10/witches-of-venice .html.

121. Venezia-tourism.com, "Witches Regatta," accessed May 29, 2022, https://www .venezia-tourism.com/en/venice-events/witches-regatta.html.

long skirts, mobcaps, and crocheted shawls to be lowered into the Grand Canal in their lightweight mascaretas—vessels that are normally raced only by women and girls. The twig brooms, stuck bristles-up near the prows, leave no doubt as to the rowers' mission. The Befanas' goal: the giant stocking hanging from the Rialto Bridge.[122] When the witches cross the finish line, the sweets in the stocking are distributed to the children in the crowd while the winner is given a glass of mulled wine and a red pennon with a picture of the bridge and a broomstick-riding witch inside a crescent moon.

When the rise of the Corona virus forced the city to cancel the regatta, eligible participants raced anyway, in full witchety drag, even though there was no giant stocking and no mulled wine waiting for them at the finish line.

The Original Pepper Cookie?

In his 2007 book *The Taste of Conquest*, Michael Krondl identifies the mildly sweet, peppery peverino cookie as a throwback to Venice's medieval heyday when there were more spices in everything and little distinction between savory and sweet. When Krondl was writing, peverini were "sold in every Venetian *Pasticceria.*"[123] Krondl interviewed Venetian baker Franco Colussi who made the cookies only occasionally, demand for these antiquated cookies having fallen off. As far as I can tell, Colussi no longer makes peverini, but the Pasticceria Costantini on the island of Murano does. I have never been to Venice, so I have never tasted peverini, and the Pasticceria Costantini

---

122. "Regatta of Befana," accessed October 6, 2022, https://www.venice-tourism .com/en/regatta-befana.

123. Krondl, *The Taste of Conquest*, 32.

website lists only the ingredients, not the secret recipe, but I have done my best.

Peverini

Ingredients

⅓ cup (47 grams) Zante currants

¼ cup marsala (38 milliliters) or other sweet red wine (enough to cover currants)

¼ cup (35 grams) pine nuts

2 cups (240 grams) flour

3 tablespoons yellow cornmeal

1½ tablespoons cocoa powder

1 teaspoon black pepper

½ teaspoon cinnamon

½ teaspoon nutmeg

½ teaspoon cumin

Pinch salt

1 cup (198 grams) sugar

¼ cup (85 grams) molasses

2 eggs, beaten

Soak the currants in the wine overnight.

Chop the pine nuts. Pine nuts are slippery little fellows. Just keep chopping until you can't see any more whole ones. Set aside.

Combine the flour with the pine nuts and other dry ingredients. Set aside.

In a small pot, heat the sugar and molasses until the sugar is dissolved. (You will still see some graininess.)

Drain the currants. (Reserve the wine to add to your pan-forte.)

Make a well in the dry ingredients and pour in the sugar/molasses mixture, stirring well. Dough will be very dry and crumbly. Add the eggs to make a stiff dough. Work in the currants.

Scoop or pinch off a tablespoonful of dough at a time and form a ball with damp hands. Pat the balls flat on a cookie sheet and bake at 375 F (190 C) for twelve to fourteen minutes or until the tops feel firm. Remove from sheets right away or they will stick even to baking parchment.

Makes forty-five cookies.

Enjoy your peverini with the rest of the wine in the bottle.

Chapter Nine

Run, Run, as Fast as You Can

The poem "The Gingerbread Boy" was first published in 1875 in *St. Nicholas*, an American children's magazine. The St. Nick connection is coincidental; our boy appeared in the May issue, and there is nothing particularly Christmassy about his flight from the kitchen and gruesome demise in the jaws of a fox. Tales of fleeing food are older than the English language, entering Europe in the mists of prehistory as part of the Indo-European cultural package. There is nothing to associate such tales with the winter solstice, so how did the runaway gingerbread boy, or his more mature counterpart, the gingerbread man, become America's Christmas mascot?

North America's Dutch settlers may have celebrated the Feast of St. Nicholas with pepernoten and speculaas, but if they did, the practice died out after New Amsterdam became New York. One thing the Dutch *did* impart was the word *koekje*, "little cake," which became the American English *cookie*. The early American gingerbread, both hard and soft, came not from the Netherlands but from England, a country whose gingerbread tradition began in the Middle Ages. English gingerbread, for the most part, called for rose water instead of orange peel and contained far fewer spices than

Lebkuchen or speculaas, concern for appearance sometimes overriding flavor.

The word *gingerbread* comes from Old French *gimgiber*, which had nothing to do with bread. The first "gingerbread" was simply a slice of candied gingerroot, the form in which it first arrived in England having wended its way from Constantinople, one of the Silk Road's western termini, along with the first dribbles of silk and tea.[124] Even in the modern refrigerator's crisper drawer, gingerroots don't last very long, and I don't suppose any fresh specimens could have survived the trip overland from India's Malabar coast.

A fifteenth-century recipe for "gyngerbrede" calls for honey, pepper, breadcrumbs, cinnamon, and cloves but, surprisingly, no ginger.[125] Perhaps the recipe's author thought that adding ginger went without saying? Cut into squares, this gyngerbrede actually sounds a lot more like the ancient Italian panforte than anything resembling our Christmas gingerbread man.

Gingerbread "fairings" were sold at English market fairs from the 1100s until the 1800s, a tradition that survives in the Cornish "fairing," a round, golden to dark brown cookie (British "biscuit") with a cracked top. Gingerbread fairings were sold throughout the year, their shapes changing to fit the season.[126] Like many of the treats and trinkets sold at English fairs, they weren't considered to be of the highest quality, and *gingerbread* soon came to mean the same as *tawdry*, a word first applied to the cheap lace collars sold at St. Audrey's Fair in Ely.

124. Tori Avey, "The History of Gingerbread," PBS, December 20, 2013, https://www .pbs.org/food/the-history-of-gingerbread/history-gingerbread/.

125. A Dollop of History, "Medieval Gyngerbrede," December 11, 2018, https:// historydollop.com/2018/12/11/medieval-gyngerbrede/.

126. Avey, "The History of Gingerbread."

Recipe

GINGERBREAD FAIRINGS

Ingredients

½ cup (113 grams) butter, softened

1 cup (198 grams) sugar

1 egg

3 tablespoons golden syrup (a.k.a. treacle) or Grafschafter
  sugar beet syrup

2 cups (240 grams) flour

1 teaspoon baking soda

2 teaspoons ginger

½ teaspoon cinnamon

Cream the butter and sugar together. Beat in the egg and stir
in the syrup.

Mix the dry ingredients and add them to the butter mixture to make a soft dough.

Shape the dough into balls a tablespoonful at a time. Place
them on the baking sheet at least two inches apart—they will
spread!

Bake your fairings at 350 F (177 C) for ten minutes or until
golden. Let them cool a little before taking them off the pan.

Makes forty cookies.

Gingerbread Spells

Meanwhile, English royals were performing their own gingerbread experiments, a process helped along by the increasing
availability of sugar. King Henry II, writing to the mayor of the
market town of Winchester in 1226, inquired if three pounds
of "Alexandrian sugar" was too much to ask for. Less than

twenty years later, Henry III was able to acquire three hundred pounds of imported "rock sugar," probably from Antwerp. By the mid 1500s, England had its own refineries for processing brown sugar into the crystalline "white," "rose," and "violet" sugars it craved.[127]

The ease with which sugar could now be gotten made the mid-sixteenth century the ideal time for Queen Elizabeth I to invent the gingerbread man, as some food historians claim she did. While the Virgin Queen did present important dinner guests with their own gingerbread doppelgangers, it was not an entirely original idea.[128] Kings and queens on the continent had long been commissioning molds in their own likenesses to celebrate their weddings and coronations. A mold carved to look like a particular monarch could be used throughout that monarch's reign, but I doubt even Queen Elizabeth would have splurged on a mold that would be used for just one dinner party. Elizabeth's gingerbread men, if we can call them that, were probably shaped by hand, sheets of gold leaf stuck on with icing made of the increasingly large amounts of sugar in the royal sugar barrels. Gilt gingerbread letters were also served at court, in case any of the guests hadn't already learned their alphabet.

For most of its history, Lebkuchen was either not iced at all or was given a glaze so thin you hardly noticed it, but the cheaper sugar became, the less bakers regarded it as a spice

127. Mintz, *Sweetness and Power*, 82. The source doesn't say, but I assume the latter two were infused with rose water and violets.

128. Barbara Rolek, "The History of Gingerbread," The Spruce Eats, November 10, 2019, https://www.thespruceeats.com/the-history-of-gingerbread-1135954#:~ :text=The%20first%20gingerbread%20man%20is,became%20a%20token%20 of%20love.

to be used sparingly and the more they slathered it on. Pfeffernüsse acquired a hard white sugar shell, and bakers started decorating the large Lebkuchen hearts that still hang in German Christmas market stalls with colored frosting roses and cursive greetings. But when it comes to artfully iced cookies, the rock-hard *perničky* take the cake.

Perničky are the Czech version of gingerbread, the fine white lines of icing on top as delicate and complicated as lace. *Perničky* are so beautiful, in fact, that you won't mind that they're too hard to eat. Could these tiny works of art have been the inspiration for the painstaking gingerbread portraits at Elizabeth's court? The queen's personal astrologer, John Dee, spent several months plumbing the mysteries of the universe in the city of Prague from which, just perhaps, he brought home the idea of applying hard, white royal icing to the royal gingerbread.

In the English countryside, humbler magicians than Dee employed gingerbread figures in their spells. If a girl had no one to buy her a gingerbread fairing, she could buy herself a gingerbread "husband," the eating of which, she was promised, would produce the real thing, especially if she ate it on Halloween.[129] If she had a particular fellow in mind, all she had to do was feed him an enchanted gingerbread man, and he would be hers. If she had trouble conceiving after the wedding, she could eat a gingerbread rabbit to restore her fertility.

In the 1500s, gingerbread, like comfits—those hard, sugar-coated nuts and seeds—was still present at all happy occasions,

---

129. Alena Kate Pettitt, "Gingerbread Husbands: An Elizabethan All Hallow's Eve Recipe," The Darling Academy, October 28, 2020, https://www.thedarlingacademy.com/articles/gingerbread-husbands-a-vintage-all-hallows-eve-recipe/.

not just Christmas. Then, in 1616, as puritanical anti-Christmas clouds gathered over England, Ben Jonson included oranges, marzipan, and gingerbread in a list of New Year's gifts in *Christmas His Masque*, a piece he wrote in defense of the celebration of Christmas.[130] Still, gingerbread was not associated exclusively with Yuletide. The feast of Christmas was banned in the Puritans' Massachusetts Bay Colony, but only until 1683—not long enough for the tradition to die out even in New England. Gingerbread continued to be baked throughout the colonial period, but as a medicinal food, as it had been in the Middle Ages, not as a Christmas treat.

The Black Hessians

In my fifth grade social studies class, I was taught how George Washington slipped across the Delaware on Christmas Day to surprise the drunken Hessian mercenaries garrisoned at Trenton. We all know how the ensuing battle turned out, but how, exactly, had those hired German guns been celebrating, other than with tankards of rum, before the Americans crashed the party? The answer is: they hadn't been. Already on the alert for some kind of attack, the Hessians had been sleeping in their uniforms, muskets at the ready, their forty hogsheads of rum still unopened when the Continental forces arrived.[131]

The Hessians, I learned, weren't exactly mercenaries but soldiers in the armies of various German princes. Frederick II,

---

130. Ronald Hutton, *The Stations of the Sun* (Oxford: Oxford University Press, 1996), 23.

131. Washington Crossing Historical Park, "Were the Hessians drunk when Washington attacked Trenton?" accessed November 20, 2022, https://www.washingtoncrossingpark.org/hessians-drunk/#:~:text=We've%20all%20heard%20the,myth%20rather%20than%20documented%2Ofact.

Prince of Hessen-Cassel, got seven pounds sterling, four shillings for each of the eighteen thousand soldiers he rented out, but the soldiers themselves got little more than rations, muskets, and uniforms.[132] The practice wasn't a new one. Earlier in the century, Augustus the Strong (he of the giant Stollen knife) had given an entire cavalry regiment to Prince Frederick William I of Prussia in exchange for forty-eight Chinese vases.[133]

The Hessians who were sold to the British came from principalities throughout the Holy Roman Empire, not just Hessen. And by end of the war, they weren't even all German. To make up the numbers they'd lost to disease on the trip across the Atlantic and in battle, the Hessian regiments recruited both free and enslaved Black men to fight with them. The free men were more likely to be welcomed into the infantry, while escaped slaves were given jobs as cooks, laborers, and drummers.

Rather than return to a life of slavery and severe repercussions for having thrown in their lot with the British, many of these "Black Hessians" chose to accompany the returning troops to Hessen-Kassel, Waldeck, Brunswick, and other principalities to make new lives in the Old World. How many is difficult to determine. The German commanders weren't in the habit of recording the races of their troops, and almost all English names were transmuted to German, "Charles" becoming "Karl," "John" becoming "Johannes."[134] In one curious case,

---

132. PBS, "Hessians," *Liberty!: The American Revolution*, accessed October 6, 2022, https://www.pbs.org/ktca/liberty/popup_hessians.html.

133. Dawn Jacobson, *Chinoiserie*, (London: Phaidon, 1993), 98.

134. Harry Schenawolf, "Black Hessians: German Troops Enlisted Former African American Slaves in the American Revolution," April 15, 2021, https://www.revolutionarywarjournal.com/black-hessians-german-troops-enlisted-former-african-american-slaves-in-the-american-revolution/.

a "Moritz Moses" was baptized "Wilhelm" by a Hessian chaplain.[135] I'm guessing the man's name was actually Moses, and that his German comrades had nicknamed him Moritz, the German form of Maurice, as in St. Maurice, the Holy Roman Empire's favorite Black saint.

The 1240 statue of St. Maurice in Magdeburg Cathedral shows him as a sub-Saharan African man in chain mail and white surcoat. Few medieval European artists could pull off a lion with any success, but Africans were people one could expect to see, at least occasionally, in thirteenth-century Germany, and St. Maurice is depicted realistically as one of them.[136] The thirteenth century also saw the rise of the cult of the Three Kings, Caspar, Melchior, and a black-skinned Balthasar, the anniversary of their arrival in Bethlehem on January 6 serving as an excuse to make merry all over again.

Whether St. Maurice was portrayed as a "moor" because his name meant "dark-skinned," or he was called Maurice because he was a "moor" is an etymological chicken and egg we won't get into. What is clear is that, by 1240, the African Maurice had become a poster boy for the cosmopolitan appeal of Christianity. Those Black Hessians who ended up in Hessen itself were promoted to Frederick's personal elite corps, while in Brunswick, they continued in the drum corps. Whatever they did, they were probably highly visible. While the Holy Roman Empire's colonial efforts had made Black people increasingly familiar to the Germans at home, these men, hav-

135. Christian Musgrave, "Black Hessians," accessed June 16, 2022, https://blackcentraleurope.com/biographies/black-hessians-christian-musgrave/.

136. Jeff Bowersox, "St. Maurice in Magdeburg (CA. 1240)," Black Central Europe, accessed June 3, 2022. https://blackcentraleurope.com/sources/1000–1500/st-maurice-in-magdeburg-ca-1240/.

ing beaten a path to Germany all the way from the wilds of North America, were especially good PR for the Holy Roman Empire.[137]

Most of the Black Hessians had been recruited in the Carolinas. How did a white Christmas in the Holy Roman Empire compare to those they had known while they were enslaved?[138] Christmas trees weren't yet commonplace in ordinary German homes, but they were already fashionable at court where they were hung with Pfefferkuchen and thin strands of silver *Lametta* made in Nuremberg. The Brothers Grimm, who hailed from Hanau in what is today's province of Hessen, wouldn't publish their version of "Hansel and Gretel" until 1812, but gingerbread "witch's houses" would already have been displayed in shop windows and at Frankfurt's then-four-hundred-year-old Christmas Market. I hope the members of Prince Frederick's elite corps got to sample the mulled wine and other wares.

The children's song "Lasst uns froh und munter sein," in which children leave plates out on the parlor table for St. Nicholas to fill, may not yet have been written, or at least not written down, in Prince Frederick's time, but our Black Hessians may

---

137. After a few false starts, including a tiny Prussian West Indies in the 1600s, the German Colonial Empire reached its peak in 1890 with a scattering of possessions in Africa, the Pacific, and China. By 1919, it was all washed up, but its legacy lived on in the *Kolonialwarenläden*, shops that sold goods from the former colonies, such as cocoa, rice, sugar, coffee, and tea.

138. When it came to the free labor force, Christmas in the antebellum American South was celebrated much as it had been within the confines of England's feudal system: the enslaved plantation workers, much like medieval serfs, were not only allowed but encouraged to eat, drink, and be merry and even to demand gifts from the plantation owner, a one-day indulgence that was meant to keep them happy the rest of the year.

well have witnessed the practice.[139] According to *Die Lieder-fiebel*, the song was first sung in the uplands of the Rhineland-Palatinate on into the Taunus mountains north of Frankfurt. I wonder what the Black Hessians made of all these traditions, or if they got to take part in any of them. Many of the German Hessians who, after their defeat, stayed in the new United States went home first to pick up their wives and children. I have found no record of a Black Hessian who was able to bring his family with him to Germany.

General Washington's Star Baker

Not all Hessians fought for the British. In 1754, Master baker Christoph Ludwick emigrated from Giessen in the principality of Hessen-Darmstadt to Philadelphia where he would eventually run a franchise of nine gingerbread-baking houses.[140] Ludwick, we are told, brought all his equipment with him when he left Hessen-Darmstadt, and two of his dark wooden cookie molds now reside in the collection of the Museum of the American Revolution. But those two molds were certainly not made in Germany. One shows a rather dour-looking lady in antiquated, seventeenth-century dress, the other a vase of fanciful flowers.[141] Compared to the naturalistic figures the master mold carvers were producing in the Old World, Ludwick's look like Pennsylvania Dutch folk art. No doubt he did

139. Heribert and Johannes Grüger, *Die Weihnachtsliederfiebel: Laterne-, Weihnachts- und Winterlieder.* (Düsseldorf: Patmos, 2001), 8.

140. Gary Shattuck, "George Washington's 'Baker Master,'" Journal of the American Revolution, May 27, 2015, https://allthingsliberty.com/2015/05/George-washingtons-baker-master/.

141. Museum of the American Revolution, "Christopher Ludwick's Cookie Board," accessed June 26, 2022, https://www.amrevmuseum.org/collection/Christopher-ludwick-s-cookie-board.

bring his molds with him from Giessen, but as they wore out, he had new ones made by local craftsmen.

In 1776, Ludwick set aside his molds to volunteer his services to the Continental Army. At first, he was in charge of morale, haranguing would-be deserters with stories of the privations he'd suffered in his war-torn homeland—in Germany, there was always a war going on somewhere. Later, he snuck behind the Hessian lines in Staten Island to gather information, procure gunpowder, and encourage the desertion of his former countrymen. Promoted to the position of George Washington's baker-in-chief, Ludwick presented himself as a miracle worker when he turned one hundred pounds of flour into one hundred thirty loaves of bread—thirty more than George had expected. General Washington knew how to lead an army, but he had no idea how much of a loaf of bread is water and air.

Another of Ludwick's duties was to direct the setup and breakdown of portable ovens. "Continue baking as fast as you can," Washington once exhorted him in a letter.[142] When the portable ovens proved impractical, Ludwick established semi-permanent field ovens at Morristown, Trenton, Elizabeth, and Valley Forge. In the winter of 1777, he did some personal baking for Washington, for which he charged him thirteen pounds, ten shillings.[143] Was it gingerbread, as Ludwick would have learned to call his Pfefferkuchen by then, or the kind of soft gingerbread cake Washington's mother made?

142. Shattuck, "George Washngton's 'Baker Master.'"
143. Shattuck, "George Washington's 'Baker Master.'"

American Gingerbread

Mary Ball Washington's gingerbread recipe, which resurfaced in 1922, can be found in Anne Byrn's book *American Cake*. Known as Lafayette Gingerbread ever since Mary served it to the Marquis de Lafayette when he stopped by Mount Vernon in 1784, it contains golden raisins, orange peel, brandy, and four different spices—ingredients ordinary housewives would have found difficult to acquire.[144] But Mary Ball Washington was no ordinary housewife; she was the manager of a plantation. Though she no doubt smiled graciously and inclined her lace-capped head when the Marquis de Lafayette complimented her on the dessert, I doubt she baked it herself. And she most certainly didn't build the fire in the wall oven, stick her arm, Gretel-style, inside it to test the temperature, or rake out the coals before the pan went in.

Far from Mount Vernon, the ordinary American housewife would have been baking what Early American writer Sarah Josepha Hale called common gingerbread. Darker in color than Lafayette gingerbread, common gingerbread relied on brown sugar and molasses for its sweetness. For most, using brown sugar and molasses instead of white was a matter of expense, but eighteenth-century abolitionists boycotted what they termed *slave sugar* as a matter of principle. Molasses came from the same plantations as white sugar, but, as a less expensive byproduct of the refining process, it didn't go as far in lining the plantation owners' pockets, I suppose. Molasses,

144. Anne Byrn, *American Cake: From Colonial Gingerbread to Classic Layer, the Stories and Recipes behind More Than 125 of Our Best-Loved Cakes from Past to Present*, (New York: Rodale, 2016), 17.

too, was slave sugar in that it made up a large proportion of the rations issued to the workers in the sugar mills.

Eighteenth-century Philadelphians were probably glad when bakers like Christoph Ludwick set up shop, because their goods were so much fancier than what Americans could make themselves. In England, gingerbread had transitioned from a sticky, panfortelike confection to a crispy biscuit the lovelorn could buy at fairs, while in the American colonies, gingerbread often meant a plain cake baked at home.

SOFT GINGERBREAD

Ingredients

1 teaspoon baking soda

1 cup (236 milliliters) boiling water

¾ cup (168 grams) butter, softened

½ cup (106 grams) plus 2 tablespoons brown sugar

2 eggs

1 scant cup (335 grams) molasses

2¼ cups (270 grams) flour

2 teaspoons ginger

½ teaspoon allspice

Put the baking soda in a bowl. Pour in the boiling water straight from the pot. Stir and set aside to cool.

Grease and flour an eight-by-ten-inch pan. (You can use a smaller pan, but you will need to bake your gingerbread a little longer.)

Cream the butter and sugar in another bowl. Add the eggs and molasses and stir.

Stir in the flour and spices a little at a time. When mixed, add the baking soda/water mixture. Stir well and pour into the pan.

Bake at 375 F (190 C) for thirty to thirty-five minutes.

Gingerbread Afloat

Americans also baked hard gingerbread to sell in the ports where it was touted as a remedy for seasickness. The gingerbread cookies hawked at the docks, I imagine, were baked as hard as tack so they could be nibbled on long journeys as the ship pitched up and down.

The following recipe is adapted from one of the same name in Sarah Josepha Hale's 1841 cookbook, *The Good Housekeeper*.[145] The ingredients and even the terminology—the reader is told to "rub" in the butter and the sugar—is not much different from those of medieval England or from the recipe for "ginger-bread cakes" Englishwoman Hannah Glasse included in her 1747 *The Art of Cookery Made Plain and Easy*.[146] The white sugar and rose water, the absence of molasses, and the fact that the recipe comes right after "Tea Cakes" suggests that Sarah intended her hard gingerbread for guests, not the riffraff down at the docks. Still, it is quite hard.

Sarah tells us only to bake the gingerbread "in flat pans."[147] She probably cut hers into squares or wedges, like Scotch shortbread, as soon as it came out of the oven. Hard ginger-

145. Yes, *that* Sarah Josepha Hale—the one who wrote "Mary Had a Little Lamb."

146. Erin Rushing, "Holiday Cooking with Hannah Glasse," Unbound Smithsonian Library and Archives, December 14, 2021, https://blog.library.si.edu /blog/2021/12/14/holiday-cooking-with-hannah-glasse/#.Y9P-KnbMLIV.

147. Hale, *Early American Cookery*, 99.

bread is impossible to cut after it cools, so cut it into whatever manageable shapes you like *before* it goes in the oven.

Sarah does not indicate that her gingerbread, or any other recipe in her book, was meant specifically for Christmas. In fact, she doesn't mention any holidays at all, though she does include a recipe for "Wedding Cake."

Recipe

HARD GINGERBREAD

Ingredients

½ cup (113 grams) butter
⅔ cup (132 grams) sugar
1 teaspoon rose water
1 generous teaspoon milk
1⅔ cup (200 grams) flour
1 tablespoon ginger

Cream the butter and sugar. Add the rose water, milk, flour, and ginger. The dough will be very crumbly. Shape the dough into a smooth ball, adding a little more milk if needed.

Roll the dough out to ⅛-inch thickness and cut into desired shapes.

Place the cookies on a baking sheet and bake at 325 F (165 C) for ten minutes.

Let your cookies sit a few minutes before transferring them to a plate to cool.

The Journey to Christmas

How the gingerbread boy/man/husband made the jump from every day to Christmas Day can be seen most clearly in

Pennsylvania. Cookies incorporating a wide variety of spices either weren't possible in America or weren't preferred by the English-speaking colonists. The idea of gingerbread as a Christmas treat was spread by the Pennsylvania Dutch, who were actually German, not Dutch, and who came from a variety of Protestant sects, and by the Moravians, who were also, for the most part, German, or at least German-speaking. The first English-speaking colonists were mostly city dwellers who'd faced a steep learning curve as soon as they'd landed on North American shores. As a professional baker, Christoph Ludwick had probably been a city dweller, too, but many of the other early German-speaking settlers had been farmers in Saxony, Switzerland, the Rhineland, and Bohemia. They were used to growing and preparing their own food and baking their own breads and cakes for Christmas.

The people destined to become the Pennsylvania Dutch may have brought a few wooden cookie molds with them, but when those wore out, they were replaced by more simply carved ones and by tin cookie cutters. (Sarah Josepha Hale, who apparently didn't have any cookie cutters, recommends cutting the rolled-out dough for one of her "Warm Cakes for Breakfast and Tea" with a glass tumbler.)[148]

Even with the Germans' help, the gingerbread man's rise to festive prominence was hardly meteoric. The recipe below is for the kind of cookie a New Jersey housewife might have baked in the early 1800s, a time by which many Americans had only vague notions of which parts of England, Ireland, Scotland, or Germany their ancestors had come from. Pre-

---

148. Hale, *Early American Cookery*, 102.

dominantly English households may have baked gingerbread all year, Germanic ones mainly for Christmas.

In the 1700s, when most cooking was still done over an open hearth, one of the leading causes of death for women was fire, as I used to tell visitors to Madison, New Jersey's Museum of Early Trades and Crafts back when I was a docent. Had the fireplace in the museum's kitchen exhibit had an actual fire in it, I, in my modern clothing, probably wouldn't have had anything to worry about, but the eighteenth-century woman's voluminous skirts were a constant source of danger. Housewives died often and young. Because the farmstead couldn't function for long without a woman in the kitchen, men quickly remarried, their new wives bringing their own culinary preferences with them. When the wall oven came along, the old wafer iron, in which balls of dough were pressed and held in the fire one at a time, was quickly discarded in favor of the metal cookie cutter and cookie sheet.

Medieval and Early Modern recipes are vague when it comes to quantities, using terms like "a goodly amount." Hale, a progressive, takes a more scientific approach by telling us how many pounds of butter, sugar, and flour to use, but most housewives would have been measuring their ingredients with whatever china teacup they happened to have on hand, the forerunner of the modern, standardized American "cup."

In those days, sugar wasn't scooped but clipped from a "sugarloaf" using a pair of iron "sugar nips." The sugarloaf, which is shaped more like a lady's intimate toy than a cone, was the form in which white sugar was sold for hundreds of years, whether you got it from the Jordan Valley in the year 1000 or from the dry goods store down the street in nineteenth-century New Jersey. The earthenware form in which the sugar was molded had a hole in the bottom through which the molasses dripped during the last stage of the refining process. If you want to see how this works, fill a glass jar with dark brown sugar, screw the lid on tight, and leave it for a few weeks. When you come back, the sugar at the top will be fairly light, while the sugar at the bottom will be dark and sticky. In colonial days, the refinement of brown sugar into white took place in England, after which it was shipped back across the Atlantic where it was sold to the colonists.

The English gingerbread man's journey from the seasonal fair to Santa's cookie plate has been a long and haphazard one. But watch out: he might still have the energy to get up and run away. The chewy gingerbread men in the following recipe can be dressed up in icing when they're cool, or you can brush them with milk and press on currants before they go in the oven.

Gingerbread Men

Ingredients

1 cup (226 grams) butter, softened
⅔ cup (142 grams) brown sugar
1 egg, beaten
½ cup (170 grams) molasses
3½ cups (420 grams) flour plus a little more for rolling out
1½ tablespoon ginger
1 teaspoon cinnamon
¼ teaspoon ground cloves
Milk for brushing
Zante currants

For the Icing
2 egg whites
1½ cups (169 grams) powdered sugar

Cream the butter and brown sugar. Stir the egg and molasses in vigorously.

Add the flour and spices a little at a time and work into a smooth dough.

Shape the dough into a ball, wrap in plastic, and let sit at room temperature overnight.

Turn the dough onto a floured surface and roll out to ¼-inch thickness. The dough will be sticky. Go to town with your cookie cutters. Brush the cookies you're not going to ice with milk and apply the currants. Let the ones you are going to ice cool completely before icing.

Bake your gingerbread men at 350 F (177 C) for twelve to fifteen minutes.

For the icing, beat the egg whites until soft peaks form. Stir in the powdered sugar. Keep the bowl of icing covered in plastic wrap until you're ready to pipe it onto your cooled, unglazed gingerbread men.

Makes about twenty-four.

Moravian Stars

When the members of the Herrnhuter Brotherhood, a Protestant sect with roots in medieval Bohemia, emigrated to the Americas, they brought the usual Central European gingerbread recipes with them. Those who settled in North Carolina eventually refined those recipes into the "Moravian cookie," a scalloped, cardboard-thin wafer flavored with cinnamon, ginger, nutmeg, cloves, and lemon peel. Touted as the world's thinnest cookie, Moravian cookies are tricky to pull off at home without burning them. (Fortunately, you can buy them: Dewey's Bakery in Winston-Salem has been selling them since 1930.)[149]

Even more famous than the Moravian cookie is the Moravian star, which is not to eat. A genuine "Moravian" or "Herrnhut" star is composed of seventeen four-sided points and eight three-sided points.[150] Even after you've acquired the genuine article from the Herrnhuter Brotherhood in Saxony, as the church is still known in Germany, chances are you'll have to assemble it yourself, a task which can take more than an hour.

Outside Germany, the Brotherhood is known as the Moravian Church. It was from Moravia and Bohemia that members of the Unitas Fratrum, followers of Czech church reformer Jan Hus (burned at the stake in 1415), fled to escape religious persecution by the ruling Catholic Habsburgs. In Saxony, they found shelter with Count Nikolaus Ludwig von Zinzendorf und Pottendorf (1700–1760), a thoughtful young man who liked to write love letters to Jesus and toss them out his bedroom window. It was Ludwig, as he was known to his followers, who established the Moravian community in Pennsylvania before returning to die in Saxony. (Ludwig also spent time in the Danish West Indies where he tried, unsuccessfully, to talk the plantation masters out of their slave-holding ways.)

149. Dewey's Bakery, "The Dewey's Bakery Story," accessed November 6, 2022, https://deweys.com/pages/our-history.

150. Herrnhut, "Herrnhuter Sterne: The origin of the Christmas stars," accessed January 25, 2023, https://www.herrnhuter-sterne.de/en/. One of the triangular points is sometimes left off to leave room for the cable by which the star is suspended.

Because the Moravian missionaries were often sent to dangerous places, their children were brought up in the boarding school back in Herrnhut, where they were taught to make three-dimensional stars as part of their geometry lesson. Lit from within, the stars represent the Star of Bethlehem. The making of these stars has since become a Herrnhuter cottage industry, one with which I wouldn't dare to compete. The following paper star, which has only twelve points and takes about twenty minutes to make, is the perfect size for tying on a cookie plate or hanging on the Christmas tree.

Craft

PAPER STAR

Tools and Materials

4 small squares of paper, about 4 inches each

Scissors

Glue

Loop of thin string or metallic cord

Fold each square of paper into eighths. Unfold. Set two squares aside.

Cut one of the other two squares along the lines shown in Figure 9a. (Simply cut along the creases you have already made, but don't cut all the way to the middle.)

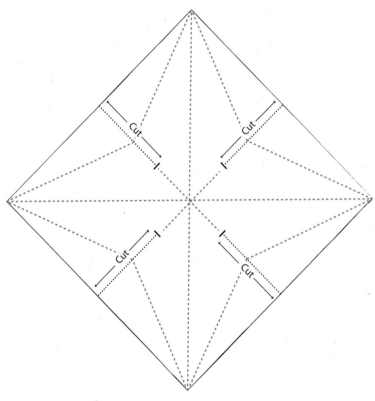

Figure 9a

Fold each of the cut edges to the center line as in Figure 9b.

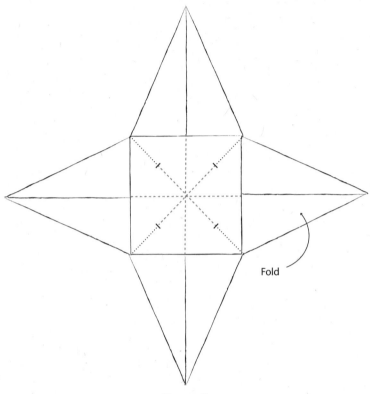

Figure 9b

Slide the flaps one over the next and glue in place to make four triangular points. Now you have a four-pointed star that's flat on one side (Figure 9c).

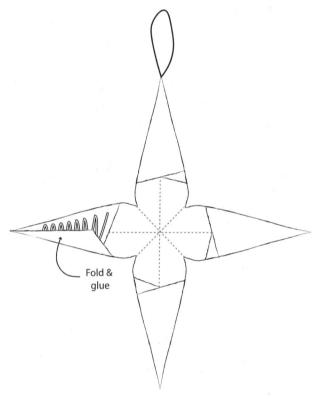

Fold &
glue

Figure 9c

Repeat the above steps with the second square of paper to make a second four-pointed star.

But wait! Before you glue the last flap down, secure your loop of string inside the point.

Cut the remaining two squares of paper into four squares each. Fold and glue each square to make a total of eight points (Figure 9d).

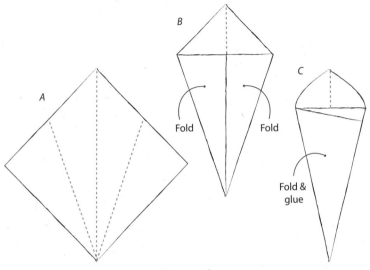

Figure 9d

Glue your two four-pointed stars back-to-back (Figure 9e).

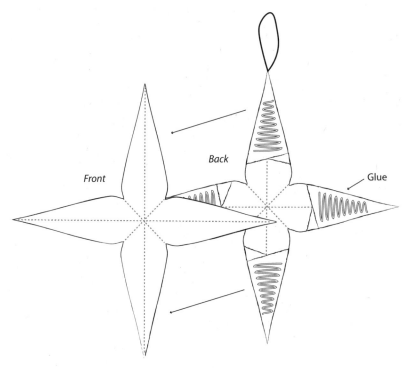

Figure 9e

Apply a little glue to the open edges of each of the eight free-floating points and glue to each side of the four-pointed star to make a twelve-pointed star (Figure 9f). Give the glue time to dry well at each stage of production.

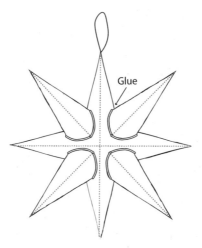

Figure 9f

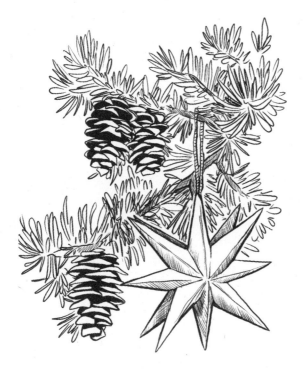

Chapter Ten
Stirring Things Up

ost of the foods at Queen Elizabeth I's Christmas court would have tasted unfamiliar to us: mincemeat pies in which meat still played a starring role and "plum porridge": prunes and raisins steeped in beef broth, a precursor of plum pudding. Years ago, I mentioned to a British coworker that I was thinking of making a plum pudding for Christmas. She advised me not to. There was much too much chopping, too much steam, and too much suet involved for what, in her opinion, was a fairly low return. Besides, it was already mid-December, which meant it was too late to start making pudding.

In England, the last Sunday before Advent is Stir-Up Sunday, when fruits and nuts are chopped and, yes, stirred, to make the traditional Christmas pudding. But that's not where the name comes from—at least, not officially. The sermon the Book of Common Prayer prescribes for this day includes the exhortation, "Stir up, we beseech thee, O Lord, the wills of the faithful people, that they, plenteously bringing forth the fruit of good works, may of thee be plenteously rewarded."[151] Once those fruits, nuts, and suet are chopped and stirred, they're steamed. In the old days, this took place in a cloth bag; nowadays, the batter is poured into a mold. Once it's cooked, the pudding is put away to mature, after which it's topped with a sprig of holly and iced on Christmas Day. There isn't always a clear line between Christmas pudding, which is made in a mold like a cake, and Christmas cake, which is sometimes steamed like a pudding before baking.

Each December, another coworker, who was French, would ask me to keep my eyes open for her favorite fruitcake at the A&P supermarket in my neighborhood.[152] Not the one from Anne Page, A&P's own brand, she was careful to specify, or the Old Fashion Claxton Fruit Cake, which is shipped from Georgia; she wanted the Jane Parker fruitcake, which could only be bought at A&P. The A&P supermarket chain is no more, so when I recently found Jane Parker fruitcakes available online, I assumed they were leftovers that had been baked before the supermarket's demise in 2015. But the beloved brand has, in fact, been revived. I'm sure my friend, who has since passed on, would be pleased.

151. The Church of England, "The Twenty-Fifth Sunday after Trinity," accessed January 25, 2023, https://www.churchofengland.org/prayer-and-worship /worship-texts-and-resources/book-common-prayer/collects-epistles -and-gospels-70.

152. The Great Atlantic and Pacific Tea Company (1856–2015), in whose bakery section my immigrant Saxon grandfather worked for much of his adult life, was one of the few American grocery stores that could be relied on to stock imported Bahlsen Pfefferkuchen at Christmastime. There's a lot of history in grocery store names. Grand Union, another American chain, was founded in 1872 as the Jones Brothers Tea Company, and hiding in name of the German chain EDEKA is "Einkaufsgenossenschaft der deutschen Kolonialwarenhändler," an association of merchants dealing in colonial goods.

As for the Claxton fruitcake, it's a southern Christmas specialty that's still going strong. I had assumed it was baked from an old Claxton family recipe brought over from England in the time of King George. I was wrong. The Claxton company was founded in 1910 by immigrant Italian baker Savino Tos who, after passing through the sleepy town of Claxton, Georgia one summer, decided to open a bakery there. Tos had no children, and when he died, the company passed to his employee, Albert Parker.[153] Parker is not an uncommon name, so it's not likely he was related to Jane, whose own geographic origins are unclear: according to the Jane Parker website, their fruitcakes are "proudly baked in America's heartland."[154]

Why did my French friend prefer Jane Parker's to Claxton's or even to the not-too-bad fruitcake the snack cake baker Hostess produced for a while? The obvious answer is that she thought Jane Parker's tasted better. Or maybe she didn't like the look of those green-dyed cherries Claxton puts in theirs. More likely, she associated a specific set of memories with the particular blend of fruits, nuts, and spices that is a Jane Parker fruitcake. Whatever the reason, fruitcake brand loyalty is serious business in America. The fact that most Americans now buy their fruitcake instead of baking it at home is in keeping with the oldest of Old World Christmas confectionary tradition, when marzipan, lebkuchen, and other spiced sweetmeats were doled out by the apothecaries or baked by strictly ruled guilds.

---

153. Claxton Fruitcake, "The Claxton Story … It's All About Family!" accessed June 14, 2022, https://claxtonfruitcake.com/about-us.

154. "Frequently Asked Questions," accessed January 25, 2023, https://janeparker.com/pages/faqs.

Homemade fruitcake, which was originally a wedding and special occasion cake, beat gingerbread to the American Christmas table by at least a hundred years. I'm sure plenty of Americans were eating gingerbread for Christmas by the time Ruth Berolzheimer put together the 1940 edition of *The American Woman's Cook Book*, but she lists only "Christmas fruit cake," "Georgia Christmas pudding," and "quick Christmas relish" under "Christmas" in the index. Berolzheimer does include recipes for three different kinds of soft gingerbread, gingersnaps, and "gingernuts," but she doesn't associate any of them with Christmas. She may have been of the opinion that all cookies were Christmas cookies, the only difference being that, in December, one bakes them in greater quantities and varieties, an attitude many Americans take today. (Soft gingerbread was once baked for weddings, but as Americans prospered, it gave way to the heavier, more labor-intensive fruitcake with its quantities of expensive, imported dried fruits.)

The giant fruitcake or "great cake" with which Martha Washington welcomed her husband home for Christmas 1797 was more like a raisin cake than what we think of as a fruitcake today. The only fruits in it were dried currants, which may have been all Martha could get at the time. The idea of a heavier cake in which roughly chopped fruits and nuts took the lead was reintroduced to America by later immigrants from Ireland, where fruitcake baking is begun a month or more before Christmas. Some Irish cottages even have a special niche in an outside wall where the brandy-anointed cake can be kept while it matures. The last step before Christmas is to cover the cake, like Queen Victoria's wedding cake, in marzipan and royal icing whitened with—please don't try this at home—laundry bluing.[155]

Today's North American fruitcake has shed her almond and sugar petticoats and changed from a round cake to a ring or easily shipped rectangular loaf. The prunes that distinguished the English "plum" cake have been replaced by black raisins, and the Georgia pecan has now joined the Old World almond, sometimes even shouldering it out of the picture entirely. And what about those dyed red and green glacé cherries? In early America, candied fruits were costly imports, so the more visible they were, the better.

In the recipe below, I've combined Ruth Berolzheimer's 1938 "Christmas Fruitcake" with a few touches from Sarah Josepha Hale's 1841 "Rich Plum or Wedding Cake." Sarah, who was born in 1788, briefly taught at a private school in New Hampshire before her mother died and she had to help her father, a Revolutionary War veteran, run the family inn. Thanks to her brother Horatio, who brought home textbooks for his little sister to read, Sarah received a vicarious Dartmouth education and went on to write novels and poems and to edit the fashionable magazine *Godey's Lady's Book*, work with which she supported herself and her five children after her husband died.[156]

Sarah, I imagine, celebrated Christmas in proper Protestant American fashion, with an orange, a penny, and a square of hard gingerbread stuffed into a sock for each child. But I'm curious to know to what extent, if any, Ruth Berolzheimer

155. Rena Moran, *Christmas in Ireland* (Chicago: World Book, 1985), 72.

156. Janice (Jan) Bluestein Longone, "Introduction to the Dover Edition," in *Early American Cookery: "The Good Housekeeper," 1841* by Sarah Josepha Hale (Mineola, NY: Dover Publications, 1996), vi.

celebrated Christmas. Born Theresa Ruth Berolzheimer in 1886, she founded a Hebrew School in Chicago Heights at the age of seventeen, and by the age of twenty-two had earned a degree in chemical engineering. She worked mainly as a social worker before editing *Good Eating* magazine. She never married. According to her nephew Henry, who worked for her for a time, she was "kind of a lousy cook," but *The American Woman's Cookbook* soon became a classic and was the only English language cookbook in the house where I grew up.[157]

Sarah Josepha Hale advises her readers to "stone" the raisins, but it looks like by 1938, Americans had gotten used to crunching the seeds. I'm not sure what Sarah means when she calls for "sweetmeats cut small," but I think dates will do.[158] So as not to overpower Sarah's rose water or orange flower water, I have replaced Ruth's cold coffee (a vestige of the ancestral lekach?) with cold tea. Neither Ruth nor Sarah advocate pecans or cherries, but I have put them in anyway.

Because I'm not expecting you to feed an army, or Queen Victoria's wedding party, I've cut Ruth's recipe in half.

Recipe

AMERICAN CHRISTMAS FRUITCAKE

Ingredients

1 cup (226 grams) butter, softened

1¾ cups (481 grams) brown sugar

2¾ cups (330 grams) flour

157. Mike Sula, "Omnivorous: The Cookbook Queen: The story of a lost Chicago culinary empire and its guiding force, Ruth Berolzheimer," September 11, 2008, https://chicagoreader.com/food-drink/omnivorous-the-cookbook-queen/.

158. Hale, *Early American Cookery*, 100.

1 teaspoon nutmeg
½ teaspoon mace
¼ teaspoon cloves
1 teaspoon cinnamon
½ teaspoon baking soda
1½ teaspoons baking powder
4 cups (596 grams) black raisins
2¾ cups (111 grams) Zante currants
1⅓ cups (226 grams) citron or lemon peel chopped fairly fine
¾ cups (105 grams) dates, chopped
½ cup (100 grams) glacé cherries
5 eggs, well beaten
½ cup (170 grams) molasses
½ cup (114 milliliters) cold black tea
¼ cup (57 grams) rose water or orange flower water
Juice and zest of 1 medium orange
Juice and zest of ½ lemon
½ cup (170 grams) quince jelly
½ cup (57 grams) chopped pecans
Whole pecans to top

In a very large bowl, cream butter and sugar. Beat in eggs. Add orange and lemon zests.

In another large bowl, mix flour, baking soda, baking powder, and spices. Stir in raisins, currants, dried citron or lemon peel, dates, and chopped pecans. Add this mixture to butter mixture, alternating with molasses, tea, juices, and jelly.

Pour into greased and floured tube pan or two loaf pans.

Arrange whole pecans in pattern on top. Put a pan of water on oven rack under the cake and bake at 300 F (150 C) for two hours.

The Mysterious Malinda Russell

Amelia Simmons published the first American cookbook in 1796, but in 1862, just a year after the end of the American Civil War, professional pastry chef and entrepreneur Malinda Russell (1812–?) self-published one of the very first cooking memoirs, *Domestic Cookbook: Containing a Careful Selection of Useful Receipts for the Kitchen.* What Malinda hadn't learned from studying other cookbooks of the times she'd been taught by Fanny Steward, whom she described in the introduction as "a colored cook of Virginia."[159] Malinda, the daughter of a freed slave from Tennessee, doesn't tell us anything else about Fanny or how she came to know her, but if Fanny had been working as a cook in Virginia before the Civil War, it's quite possible that she had been a slave.

We don't know what happened to Fanny, and we don't know what happened to Malinda beyond the publication of her book. She had been saving up money to emigrate with her disabled son to Liberia, but it's more likely that they both died in the 1866 fire that swept through the small town in Michigan where they had been living. The same fire destroyed all but one copy of *Domestic Cookbook*, which now resides at the University of Michigan.[160]

With recipes for gingerbread, custard, fruitcake, Dover cake, and Queen's Party Cake, *Domestic Cookbook* reflects the

159. Museum of Food and Drink, "Fanny Steward," accessed January 25, 2023, https://legacyquiltproject.mofad.org/quilt/fanny-steward/.

160. Burton, Monica, Osayi Endolyn, and Toni Tipton-Martin, "The Legacy of Malinda Russell, the First African-American Cookbook Author," February 23, 2021, https://www.eater.com/22262716/malinda-russell-author-a-domestic-cookbook.

distinctly English heritage of Southern baking, as well as the skill and knowledge of those who did the work.

The Quintessential Christmas Cake

Can any one cake be called the quintessential Christmas cake? Of course not. But if I had to name just one recipe that embodies the whole of Christmas baking history, both the dark chapters and the bright, it would be the Caribbean Black Cake. Containing a longer, only slightly more tropical list of ingredients than Malinda's nineteenth-century Southern American "Fruit Cake,"[161] Black Cake is both a close cousin of Queen Victoria's wedding cake and the sort of cake that could only have come about in the ethnic melting pot of the Caribbean.

I first heard of Black Cake at a friend's backyard barbecue. I can't remember how we got onto the subject, but another guest at the barbecue, United States Air Force Veteran Wayne G, told me a story about how, as a child growing up in San Fernando on the island of Trinidad, he got into trouble for breaking into his godmother's stash of Black Cakes. It wasn't just that he'd breached the tins before Christmas; Black Cake has enough alcohol in it that overindulging can make you tipsy.

When I delved into the particulars of Black Cake making, many of the steps sounded familiar. Here we were grinding almonds and soaking raisins in rum, like I had for Dresdner *Christstollen*, and the macerating of the fruits reminded me

---

161. The only fruits Malinda's calls for are raisins, currants, and citron. Mrs. Malinda Russell, *Domestic Cookbook: Containing a Careful Selection of Useful Receipts for the Kitchen* (Paw Paw, Michigan: Published by the author, 1866), 8, https://www.google.com/books/edition/A_DomesticCook_Book/jtKETYEMe pAC?hl=en&gbpv=1.

of my Lübecker grandmother's *Rumtopf* (rum pot) recipe.[162] Black Cake remains a Caribbean Christmas specialty—even those who have left the islands say it just wouldn't be Christmas without it—but it's also served, iced, at Easter and at weddings. The marzipan layer underneath the white icing, I learned, is to prevent the sugar from being absorbed by the cake.

That a Caribbean Christmas cake should contain sugar and rum made perfect sense to me, but I was surprised to see the same candied peel, currants, and paradisical spices I knew from my own family's recipes—until I remembered that some of those spices are much farther from home in the German kitchen then they are in the Caribbean kitchen.

Wayne is Black, with a little Chinese, and his neighbors in San Fernando were Indian, Irish, Chinese, and Portuguese. As the character Marble Martin states in Charmaine Wilkerson's novel *Black Cake*, "We cannot always say at which point one culture ends and another begins ... especially in the kitchen."[163]

Black cake varies from island to island and family to family. Wayne's sister attended the titular school of the *Naparima Girls' High School Cookbook*, which Wayne also encouraged me to consult. When it comes to the milling of the fruits, however, Wayne and the classic cookbook part ways. The Naparima Girls say to grind them after soaking them in the rum; Wayne insists on grinding them beforehand. Because

---

162. To make a *Rumtopf* (Low German *Rumpott*), cherries, raspberries, strawberries, plums, and other seasonal fruits are layered in a jar with a loose-fitting lid in the order they become available, starting in early spring, and covered with rum and sugar. Raisins go in last. By Christmas, the Rumtopf is ready to be eaten by the spoonful and the sweet, fruit-infused rum drunk from a glass. Unlike the fruits for Black Cake, Rumtopf is never stirred.

163. Charmaine Wilkerson, *Black Cake* (New York: Ballantine Books, 2022), 250–251.

I was anxious to get my fruits "in the drink," I did not grind them beforehand. The only advantage in doing so, that I can see, is to shorten the soaking time. The Naparima Girls say you can soak your fruits for as little as two days, but most bakers recommend at least a few months, if not a whole year. I soaked mine for one month, stirring the contents once a day to make sure all the fruits got their fair share of rum. Though I don't particularly like the smell of rum, I came to look forward to this daily ritual, and I can see why many Caribbean bakers always have at least one jar going.

Here are some more of Wayne's tips for a better Black Cake: the fruits and almonds should be ground as fine you can possibly manage (either before or after soaking). Don't screw the lid on the jar where your fruits are soaking; lay a plate or board over the mouth of the jar instead. Better for the cover to be blown off than for the jar to explode! When it comes to the batter, if a wooden spoon can stand up in it, you have achieved the proper consistency. Don't wrap your finished cake in aluminum foil: the alcohol will eat it. And lastly, Wayne warns that Black Cakes should be hidden from "people like my younger self!"

By the time the cake comes out of the oven, it's quite rummy enough for me, but many people continue to anoint it with alcohol until it's served days or weeks later. Wayne tells me that if I make a hole in the middle of the cake and keep pouring in rum, it will last *for years*. I've decided to take his word for it.

The following recipe calls for rum, but you can also use cherry brandy, Guinness, port, or a combination thereof. As for which kind of rum, use whichever kind you won't mind drinking if there's some left over. (Makes one cake.)

BLACK CAKE

To Prepare Ahead of Time

1 cup (149 grams) pitted prunes, cut up

1¾ cups (482 grams) black raisins

½ cup (72 grams) dried black cherries

½ cup (72 grams) pitted dates, cut up

¼ cup (42 grams) candied orange peel

¼ cup (42 grams) candied lemon peel

1 375-milliliter bottle rum

Soak fruits in enough rum to cover for two days at the very least, adding more rum as needed and stirring up from bottom daily.

On Baking Day

10 tablespoons butter, softened

¾ cup (50 grams) sugar

3 eggs, beaten

1 teaspoon almond extract

1 teaspoon vanilla extract

Zest of one lime

¼ cup (21 grams) almond flour

1¼ cups (150 grams) flour

1 teaspoon baking powder

½ teaspoon cinnamon

¼ teaspoon nutmeg

¼ teaspoon allspice

1½ cups (319 grams) dark brown sugar

⅓ cup (78 milliliters) boiling hot water

Grind the soaked fruits in a blender to make a wet paste. If needed, add a little rum to make blending easier.

Cream the butter and sugar together. Stir in the eggs, extracts, lime zest, and almond flour.

In a separate bowl, mix the flour, baking powder, and spices.

Stir the dry flour mixture into the butter mixture. Add the ground fruits. Set aside.

In a small pot, heat the brown sugar on very low heat, moving it around with a wooden spoon. The sugar will slowly melt and turn the color of caramel. Keep heating and stirring until it starts to buck and heave and release vents of steam. Add boiling hot water SLOWLY. If you add it too fast, you will end up with a stovetop volcano. ("Don't set the kitchen afire," Wayne had warned me shortly before. I had laughed. Five minutes later, when the stove was spattered with molten sugar, I wasn't laughing anymore.)

Continue to simmer, stirring, about five minutes. Keep it bubbling. The resulting "browning" will be thinner than molasses at first but should still coat the spoon. Set aside to cool a little.

Line a nine- or ten-inch layer cake or springform pan with baking parchment.

Put a pan of water on the bottom rack of the oven and turn to 275 F (140 C).

Pour your browning into your batter and stir well. If the browning has become too thick and sticky, heat it up again and it will thin.[164]

---

164. Instead of washing the browning pot right away, Wayne recommends cooking some chicken in it along with some Jamaican jerk seasoning and "roucou" (annatto derived from the seeds of the achiote tree, a Caribbean native).

Pour the batter into the pan and bake for three hours.

Store the cooled cake in a sealed container until ready to serve.

Deathless in Paradise

Of all the ingredients we've covered, sugar is perhaps the one with the darkest history and the bitterest legacy. The enslaved plantation workers in the Caribbean were made to churn out sugar like no one had ever churned out anything before. They were literally worked to death, many not even surviving their teens.

The zombie, a distinctly Haitian entity, is a tragic figure born of Europe and America's insatiable demand for sugar. Rather than an animated corpse that rose from the grave to terrorize the living, he was simply a slave, a person who, while technically alive, was allowed no other purpose than to work. In a less imperfect world, one might have expected the concept of the zombie to have died with Haitian independence, achieved after thirteen years of bloody revolution, but, because of the massive financial penalties France imposed on the new nation, the pace of the work barely slowed.

The word *zombie* has several possible etymologies from several West African languages, all relating to death, a corpse, the spirit of a dead person, or the god of death. An animated corpse is only the fourth definition of the word *zombie* in my 1960 *Webster's New Twentieth Century Dictionary*. The third is the power that animates the corpse, the second "any voodoo snake deity," and the first the West African Python deity. How our concept of the zombie has changed, at least in American pop culture!

In her *Encyclopedia of Witches and Witchcraft*, Rosemary Ellen Guiley defines a zombie as a "dead person brought back to life by a magician, but not to the life the person previously knew," which is how, I imagine, those West Africans must have felt after they were torn from their families, shackled in the coffinlike hold of a ship, and "released" to work themselves into the final release of the grave, a place from which they hoped fervently not to have to return.[165]

Do I want you to think of all this while you're creaming your butter and refined sugar or heating your molasses? Of course not. Well, maybe a little. At the very least, I would like your thoughts to drift, however briefly, beyond the coziness of your twenty-first-century kitchen.

---

165. Rosemary Ellen Guiley, *Encyclopedia of Witches and Witchcraft*, Second Edition (New York: Checkmark Books, 1999), 390.

Chapter Eleven

A Christmas Kitchen Herbal

We've spent a lot of time on the big guns Lebkuchen, gingerbread, and fruitcake, but there are a few more recipes I'd like to impart and a few more ingredients whose stories I want to tell. The first Old World "herbals"—illustrated directories of healing plants—were written in ancient Egypt, China, and India. When the Spanish arrived in Mexico, they were quick to commission herbals featuring the New World's unique flora, but even before that, the Maya and Aztecs were consulting their own herbals written on bark paper and cloth.

The art of the herbal flourished during the Middle Ages, both in the Arab and the Christian worlds. At first, these handwritten manuscripts were for the use of apothecaries and physicians alone, but after Johannes Gutenberg introduced movable type to Europe in the 1400s, these books became affordable enough that the layperson could keep one at home. Just as those herbals made no distinction between herb and spice, medicine and sweet, the following ingredients are bound only by their association with Christmas and my desire to tell you more about them.

Thanks to the illustrations on the jars of spices and boxes of extract we buy in the grocery store, most people know that cinnamon is the bark of a tree and vanilla the "bean" or fruit of an orchid. Fewer people are aware that peppercorns grow on a vine, that cloves are dried flower buds, or that the vanilla orchid originated in the jungles of Mexico. In North America, the blend known as pumpkin pie spice has broken free from its *Cucurbita* moorings to flavor lattés and donuts, which, however they might be advertised, often have no pumpkin in them at all. Pumpkin pie gets its signature flavor not from one spice but from five: cinnamon, ginger, nutmeg, allspice, and cloves. All of them were and still are "Christmas" spices, but, with the exception of allspice, they were all consumed in Europe long before Europeans started celebrating Christmas. And before that, of course, they had their own long histories in Asia and the Middle East.

Outside the Caribbean cultures, many people assume that the powder known as allspice is a blend of "all spices"; they have no idea that it's the dried berry of a single tree, or that a "buccaneer" was originally someone who rubbed their meat with pounded allspice and hung it in the smoke of a fire on a *buccan*, a Taino word for a wooden frame used for the purpose. (The resulting "jerky" is a Quechua word.)[166] Conversely, I suspect that some of those pumpkin spice latté drinkers, if they give any thought to the matter at all, think that "pumpkin spice" originates in the pumpkin itself or has been plucked from a single source located in some holiday wonderland akin to the medievals' fragrant Paradise.

What's the point of knowing how and when those spices got into your kitchen? First of all, it's always a good idea to know what you're eating—seed or berry; bark or root? Second,

---

166. O'Connell, *The Book of Spice*, 16.

understanding what these plants are and where they came from is crucial to understanding the modern world. When it comes to the spice trade, all our ancestors had some skin in the game, and though heads no longer roll in the nutmeg groves, the ruthless desire to corner the market on a handful of trees and shrubs growing in faraway places has laid the groundwork for the societies we live in today.

Much has been said of the enslaved labor that enabled the fever dream of the preautomation sugar industry, but little attention has been paid to the skill of those enslaved workers, many of whom were brought to those plantations expressly because they already knew how to grow and process the finicky, time-sensitive sugarcane. Meanwhile, on the island of Réunion in the Indian Ocean, an enslaved boy named Edmond Albias revolutionized the way vanilla orchids were pollinated. Albias never received the acclaim he deserved while he lived. I hope that, once you've read this chapter, you'll think of him every time you tip that bottle of vanilla extract over your measuring spoon. Understanding and appreciating the origins of your ingredients adds enjoyment to the baking process and to the eating and sharing of what you've made.

The Christmas traditions of the New World are still that: new. In the Old World, the making of Christmas specialties like Lebkuchen, Stollen, and Panforte de Siena is strictly regulated; if you want that regional seal of approval, you'd better not stray too far from the standard. Americans have never been subject to guild control, but before the early settlers could start baking, they had to figure out what to do with the strange fruits, nuts, and herbs they found in their new homeland.[167] The Spaniards quickly adapted indigenous cooking methods along with local words like *buccan* and *maíz,* while the English colonists persisted in calling maize *Indian meal* and *corn,* a generic word for grain of any kind. North Americans took readily to popping flint corn over the fire, and eventually draping strings of it over their Christmas trees, steaming other varieties of *Zea Mays* into Old World–style puddings and baking it into New World *pone,* an Algonquian-derived word for bread baked in the embers of the fire.[168] But, all in all, the colonists showed little interest in the myriad ways their Algonquian neighbors dried, processed, and cooked maize. And while they recognized the value of eating native cranberries and highbush blueberries, the dried Corinthian grape remained the preferred ingredient in tea cakes long after the American Revolution.

Instead of mourning the loss of our Old World culinary and ethnobotanical traditions, Americans can take pride in the innovative cakes, pies, and cookies our ancestors, both free and enslaved, managed to put on the table. At this writing, everyday American baking is dominated by sugar, while the more complex flavors of pumpkin pie, gingerbread, and fruitcake are reserved for the holidays. I'm hoping at least a few of my American readers will be inspired to go beyond the pages of this book and try their hands at an apple pandowdy

---

167. Because they belong to the nightshade family, eggplant was at first used as a centerpiece, not a vegetable. Another nightshade, the tomato, was known as a poison apple and a wolf peach until nineteenth-century gentleman farmer Robert Gibbon Johnson consumed one publicly on the steps of New Jersey's Salem County Courthouse—at least, that's the story we tell in New Jersey!

168. Joyce White, "Virginia Corn Pone," A Taste of History with Joyce White, April 18, 2016, https://atasteofhistorywithjoycewhite.blogspot.com/2016/04 /corn-pone-in-literature-and-life.html?m=0.

or seventeenth-century cheesecake made with almonds and freshly grated nutmeg or a dark, orange-flavored, early-twentieth-century "birthday cake."

The following information is what I hesitate to call ethnobotanical "trivia," because none of it is trivial to me. There are also recipes for a handful of cakes, breads, and cookies that didn't fit neatly into the broader narrative but which Santa Claus would nevertheless be pleased to see next to his glass of milk when he visits on Christmas Eve.

Allspice
(Pimenta dioica)

The dried berries of the allspice tree taste like cinnamon, cloves, and nutmeg all rolled into one, but without the heat of the former two. Even when placed on the tongue, it is through the nose that the flavor makes itself known. Allspice was another fruit Columbus tried to pass off as Indian black pepper, which is why its full names in Spanish are *pimienta dulce*, "sweet [black] pepper," and *pimienta de Jamaica*, after the island on whose limestone hills the glossy-leaved evergreens grow. Unrelated to any of its East Indian smell-alikes, allspice is also called newspice, because it didn't arrive in European kitchens until after 1492. Allspice is one spice that has never left its native hemisphere. The ground berries in your grocery store were probably grown where they always have been: Jamaica.

The widespread-on-the-internet idea that the Maya used allspice to embalm their dead seems to have originated with a single sentence from a paper published by Estella Weiss-Krejci in 2003: "The skeleton in Tomb 19 rested on a wooden litter and was wrapped in a shroud that contained allspice leaves."[169] The sentence refers to a burial in Guatemala's Rio Azul region. In another article, the archaeologist traces the Mayan *k'an* glyph to the Maltese cross that can be seen in the cross section of a cut allspice branch. The sign *k'an* appears in Mayan hot cocoa recipes, so it makes sense to assume it denoted allspice.[170] (Weiss-Krejci has also described a cremation burial in which a Venetian glass bead was found among the ashes, telling us that Central American cities were able to tick along for a while even after the Spanish had landed in the West Indies.[171])

Ground allspice berries are one of the spices that go into Jamaican chocolate tea balls—roasted cacao beans pounded with allspice, cinnamon, and nutmeg and rolled by hand into pointed balls that actually look more like tops, which is a good thing; you wouldn't want to mistake an unsweetened chocolate tea ball for a Jamaica rum ball (see Cacao). Once they're rolled, the balls are left to harden, after which they can be grated into hot water and milk to make a "chocolate tea" to which sugar, cream, and sometimes rum are added.

169. Estella Weiss-Krejci, "The Maya Corpse: Body Processing from Preclassic to Postclassic times in the Maya Highlands and Lowlands," Research Gate, January 2006, https://www.researchgate.net/publication/273059464_The_Maya_corpse_Body_processing_from_Preclassic_to_Postclassic_times_in_the_Maya_highlands_and_lowlands.

170. Estella Weiss-Krejci, "Allspice as Template for the Classic Maya K'an Sign," *The PARI Journal* Volume XII, No. 4, Spring 2012, https://www.yumpu.com/en/document/read/7475048/allspice-as-template-for-the-classic-maya-kan-sign-mesoweb.

171. Weiss-Krejci, "The Maya Corpse."

Almond

(Prunus dulcis)

Several years after ogling those natron balls in the Penn Museum, I was perusing the pantries of the dead in the Egyptian galleries of the Metropolitan Museum of Art where I found garlands of persea leaves, baskets of raisins (or had they been grapes when they were first laid in the tomb?), and the chestnutlike fruits of the *dôm* palm, but no almonds. Almonds, which are Central Asian natives, were a rarity in ancient Egypt. Tutankhamun, who died around 1320 BCE, was given a little jar of imported almonds to take with him to the Land of the Dead, but he was probably one of the lucky few. Even in medieval Egypt, almonds were imported from Spain and elsewhere. Almonds were common in southern Europe by Roman times, and for a time they even grew along the banks of the Rhine. A few trees ended up in Britain where they bloomed nicely but had trouble fruiting in the cold.

The slightly smaller, slightly pointier bitter almond is a variant of the sweet almond and is so bitter that, if you tried to eat one on its own, you'd probably spit it out. Most people enjoy sweet almonds—unless they're allergic—but a significant number are put off by the through-the-nose taste of the bitter almonds or almond extract in marzipan. "Like bugs," one of these marzipan haters once described it to me. The recipe below pairs sliced sweet almonds with cinnamon instead of almond extract. The acquaintance who gave it to me said her Swedish-American grandmother used to bake these right after Thanksgiving.

Almond Cookies

Ingredients

½ cup (113 grams) butter, softened

⅓ cup (71 grams) brown sugar

⅓ cup (66 grams) sugar

1 egg

1¾ cups (210 grams) flour

½ teaspoon baking powder

½ teaspoon cinnamon

½ cup (43 grams) sliced almonds (skin on)

Cream the butter and sugar. Beat in the egg. Add the rest of the ingredients, mixing well. Shape the dough into a log, wrap in plastic, and refrigerate overnight.

Cut the log into ¼-inch slices and place them on a baking sheet. Bake at 375 F (190 C) for eight minutes or until lightly browned. When sealed in a tin, they will last and last.

Aniseed

(Pimpinella anisum)

Aniseed or anise is a spindly umbelliferous plant, its tiny white flowers blooming at the end of each naked umbrella rib. The ancient Romans used aniseed to flavor the *mustaceum*, a cake made of flour, wine, and cheese. Baked on a bed of laurel leaves, the *mustaceum* wasn't for everyone; the eating of it was part of the *Confarreatio*, a sacred marriage ceremony reserved for patrician brides and grooms.

These days, anise takes the lead in *bizcochitos*, "little cakes," cutout cookies that I first tasted at the Christmas festivities at

Santa Fe, New Mexico's Palace of Fine Arts. Part of the Spanish colonists' Christmas kit, bizcochitos are New Mexico's state cookie and are usually made at home rather than bought. You can substitute butter for the traditional lard, but they won't taste quite the same.

Recipe

BIZCOCHITOS

Ingredients

½ pound (226 grams) lard, room temperature

⅔ cup (66 grams) sugar

1 tablespoon ground aniseeds

2 eggs

3 cups (360 grams) flour

½ tablespoon baking powder

¼ cup (59 milliliters) orange juice

Topping

¼ cup (50 grams) sugar

½ teaspoon cinnamon

Cream the lard and sugar. Add the aniseed. Beat in the eggs.

Mix the flour with the baking powder and add it to the lard mixture a little at a time, alternating with the orange juice.

Work the ingredients into a smooth dough, shape the dough into a ball, and roll it out to ⅛-inch thickness. Cut into shapes: fluted rounds and crescents are traditional.

Bake at 425 F (220 C) for ten to twelve minutes.

While the cookies are baking, shake the sugar and cinnamon together in a jar. Sprinkle them over the cookies while still warm.

———

Springerle are anise-flavored Christmas cookies made in German-speaking lands, especially in Switzerland and the United States' Pennsylvania Dutch Country. They may have been named for the soldier on the "springing" horse pictured on some of the earliest molds. In Nuremberg, Springerle go by the name *Nürnberger Eierzucker*, "egg sugar," the pictures on top sometimes painted with food coloring.

I normally use parchment instead of greasing my cookie sheets, but for Springerle, I grease them because I like that little taste of butter on the bottom of an otherwise butterless cookie. Smaller than speculaas molds, wooden Springerle molds are easier to find in the United States, along with carved springerle rolling pins.

Recipe

SPRINGERLE

Ingredients
1 cup (198 grams) sugar
2 eggs
2 cups (240 grams) flour
Zest of one small lemon
4 tablespoons whole aniseed

In a small bowl, beat the sugar and eggs for several minutes until thick and creamy.

Stir in the flour and lemon peel.

Shape the dough into a ball and, using an ordinary rolling pin, roll out to ¼-inch thickness. If you are using a Springerle rolling pin for the next step, you will need to roll out a rectangle the same width as the rolling pin.

Lightly flour the surface of the dough and roll the springerle rolling pin across, gently pressing down. Or press whatever molds you have into the dough. Cut the cookies apart with a sharp knife.

Scatter your aniseed over a greased baking sheet. Place cookies on top an inch apart.

Reroll leftover dough and repeat.

Leave the unbaked cookies out to dry overnight.

Bake at 250 F (130 C) for twenty-five to thirty minutes. Springerle should be white, not golden.

Let cool. You can test one, but seal the others in a tin for a week at the very least so they can absorb the flavor of the aniseeds. If they have become hard when you open the tin back up, put a slice of fresh bread in with them for a day.

Apricot
(Prunus armeniaca)

The flesh of the apricot, made into jam, provides the moisture in Elisenlebkuchen, while ground apricot kernels are the foundation of persipan, a confection very similar to marzipan. *Dominosteine* (dominoes) are Christmas petit fours in which layers of persipan, apple jelly, and Lebkuchen are covered in chocolate. Apricot kernels, like bitter almonds, contain both amygdalin and cyanide and must be "debittered" before they can be used.

Bitter Orange
(Citrus aurantium)

The term *Orangeat* that occurs in German Stollen and Leb-kuchen recipes refers specifically to the candied peel of the bitter or Seville orange, which is also the source of marma-lade. The lumpy-looking bitter orange does not make for good eating, only candying. Bitter oranges, planted by the Span-ish settlers in Florida, were the first oranges grown in North America.

Black Pepper
(Piper Nigrum)

The ancient Egyptians, who probably got their peppercorns from Somali traders, liked to stuff them up the noses of the dead. Though the Romans cooked with black pepper and exchanged peppercorns at Saturnalia, their empire wasn't built on the craving for the fruit of this South Asian vine; that started with the Venetians. When the English monk, the Ven-erable Bede, died in 735, he left his spiritual brothers the gift of a box of peppercorns. Ousted by the hotter New World capsicum, black pepper is no longer used to pay rents and ran-soms, but few households are without it. (If you've been using ground pepper, throw it away and get yourself a little mill for grinding the whole corns.)

Cacao
(Theobroma cacao)

Chocolate was drunk for thousands of years before anyone thought to solidify it in bars or roll it into truffles. Ask for a cup of hot chocolate (*xocoatl*) and you're speaking Nahuatl, the language of the Aztecs. Ask for a cup of cocoa (*kakaw*) and you're speaking Mayan. Mayan nobles drank cocoa from dedicated cups inscribed with their names, the beverage poured from a great height to create an espressolike foam. One such cup in the Metropolitan Museum of Art belonged to a King B'aje Kaan Took—assuming the barista spelled his name correctly![172]

The individuals responsible for filling King B'aje's cup would have had to free the seeds from the mango-sized cacao pod, fermenting, roasting, and grinding them fine before cooking them with water, fruit, and cornmeal. Today, most cacao is grown in Africa, but the greatest diversity of cacao species are still found in its South and Central American homelands.

Step into any north German confectionary and you're sure to find packages of *Jamaica Rumkugeln*, "Jamaica rum balls," not to be confused with Jamaican chocolate tea balls. (See Allspice.) A trufflelike sweet, Rumkugeln are basically sugar, cocoa, and rum (or rum extract) bound with finely ground oats, almonds, hazelnuts, or Lebkuchen crumbs. The ones you can buy in the shop are usually rolled in chocolate sprinkles. The following recipe for *Weihnachtskonfekt*, "Christmas chocolates," is a homestyle rumball made by the ladies of Krusendorf's Church of the Holy Trinity at the very western end of the Baltic Sea.[173]

Krusendorf's congregation is descended from an earlier congregation, the ruins of whose Gothic Church of St. Catherine of

172. James Doyle, "The Drinking Cup of a Classic Maya Noble," Metropolitan Museum of Art, September 2104, https://www.metmuseum.org/blogs/now -at-the-met/2014/maya-drinking-cup.

173. *Krusendorfer Keksteller: bewählte Rezepte, gesammelt rund um den Kirchturm* (unpaginated).

Alexandria, which was probably built on an earlier pagan site, can still be seen among the long grass and thistles overlooking the sea at nearby Jellenbek. Even after St. Catherine's was abandoned in the seventeenth century, the building was left standing for some time because the steeple served as a landmark for passing ships laden, no doubt, with rum from the West Indies.

Recipe

WEIHNACHTSKONFEKT

Ingredients
¼ cup (59 milliliters) milk
3 tablespoons butter
1⅓ cup (264 grams) sugar
3 tablespoons unsweetened cocoa powder
1½ cups (133 grams) quick-cooking oats
1 tablespoon rum extract
1 teaspoon vanilla
More cocoa for rolling (optional)

Heat the milk and butter together in a large pot on low heat until the butter is melted. Still on low heat, add the sugar and cocoa, stirring until the cocoa is incorporated and the mixture is shiny. Add the oats and cook a few minutes more. Add the rum extract and the vanilla.

Let the mixture cool a few minutes. If it's still too wet to mold with your hands, let it sit longer, but keep an eye on it—it can set when you're not looking. When cool and firm enough, mold it into balls about a tablespoon and a half in size, i.e., a little larger than a marzipan potato. If you like, you can roll the still-moist balls in more cocoa powder. Put them in the refrigerator to set. After that, you can keep them outside the refrigerator in a tin.

Cardamom
(Elettaria cardamomum)

Cardamom is the third most expensive spice after saffron and vanilla, so it's really inexcusable to buy a jar of whole green cardamom pods, become frustrated with the process of peeling the pods and grinding the tiny, surprisingly hard seeds, and subsequently forget about the jar in the back of the cabinet for five years. Should this happen to you, you will be amazed by how sharp and fresh the pods still smell when, at long last, you open the jar again. In fact, the fragrance will be even stronger than the ground cardamom you broke down and bought. Lesson learned.

It's hard to miss the similarity between the cardamom-flavored nankhatai and the North German Christmas cookies known as *Hallig Knerken*. The Halligen are tiny islets rising from the *Wattenmeer*—the mudflats into which the North Sea subsides. Land in northern Germany, which was divided equally among sons, has always been scarce, which is why many young men sought their fortunes on the high seas, making rum runs to the Caribbean aboard Danish and Prussian ships. It's not improbable that a young sailor from the Wattenmeer, having no other prospects, might have hopped aboard a Dutch East Indiaman, seen the world (and no doubt a few things he wished he hadn't), and come back with a sack of sugar, a handful of cardamom pods, and the memory of, if not the recipe for, Goan nankhatai.

Hallig Knerken were hardened in the oven so that sailors could take them on board and eat them far from home. If hardened properly, I'm told, Hallig Knerken will last until Easter.

Hallig Knerken

Ingredients

½ cup butter (113 grams), softened

½ cup (99 grams) sugar

½ teaspoon vanilla extract

1 egg

1¾ cups (210 grams) flour

¼ teaspoon cardamom

½ teaspoon baking powder

Topping

¼ cup (59 milliliters) heavy cream

⅓ cup (66 grams) Hagelzucker (see Pfefferkuchen Variation 1 for instructions)

Cream the butter and sugar. Add the vanilla and beat in the egg. Add the dry ingredients and stir until you have a fairly stiff dough.

Chill the dough one hour.

Remove the dough from the refrigerator and let sit a few minutes. Form the balls a tablespoonful at a time. Roll all the dough into balls before moving on to the next step.

Pour the cream in a cup and scatter the Hagelzucker (see page 58) evenly over a dinner plate. Dip the top of a ball into the cream and gently press it, cream side down, into the sugar.

Turn it right side up on the cookie sheet. Repeat with rest of balls and bake at 350 F (177 C) for twelve to fourteen minutes or until cookies are light golden. Reduce the heat to 200 F (93 C) and bake for another two hours. Seal in a tin when cool. Makes about twenty-four.

Cinnamon

(Cinnamomum zeylanicum; Cinnamomum cassia)

Cinnamon is the name to which two species answer. Those who swear by "true cinnamon" look down their noses at the cheaper, more widely available cassia, which is probably what's in your kitchen cabinet right now. I've mentioned how the Egyptians used cinnamon as incense. The Romans did, too, Emperor Nero burning every cinnamon stick in Rome at his wife Poppaea Sabina's funeral. It was the least he could do, considering that he may have had a hand in her death.

Because I'm not fond of the overpowering scent of cinnamon, I can't help wondering if the English word *fuggy* might have originated with sixteenth-century spice trader Anton Fugger of the Augsburg Fuggers, bankers to the Holy Roman Emperor. In true Egyptian fashion, Fugger used to burn cinnamon sticks in his fireplace in winter.[174] Because Augsburg was once a Roman outpost, it's tempting to believe that the Fuggers might have been descended from an Egyptian legionnaire who escaped the martyrdom of St. Maurice's Thebans to settle in Augusta Vindelicorum, where he burned cinnamon in thanks for his deliverance from death.

Below is a traditional German recipe for *Zimtsterne*, "cinnamon stars." The dough is flourless. If you want to make

174. Metzger, *Culinaria Germany*, 439.

them completely gluten free, use powdered sugar instead of flour when you roll them out.

ZIMTSTERNE

Ingredients

3 egg whites

2 cups (227 grams) powdered sugar

1¾ cups (147 grams) ground, blanched almonds

Zest of ½ lemon

2½ teaspoons cinnamon

Flour for rolling out

Icing

1 cup (113 grams) powdered sugar

2 tablespoons milk

½ teaspoon vanilla extract

Beat the egg whites until stiff peaks form. Add the powdered sugar, almonds, lemon zest, and cinnamon. If it's not too sticky, shape the dough into a ball. If this seems impossible, let the dough sit several minutes to half an hour in the bowl.

When you're able to, form your ball and place it on a floured surface. Using floured hands, pat it flat. Apply a "skin" of flour over the surface of the dough and gently roll it out to about ¼-inch thickness. Let sit a few more minutes.

Cut out using a star-shaped cookie cutter. Gently remove the stars to a cookie sheet. You might need to slide a knife under each star to unstick it from the table. Let the cookies sit a few hours. (If you bake them right away, they will spread and look like blossoms, not stars.)

Bake at 300 F (150 C) for twenty minutes, during which time you can mix the ingredients for the icing.

Ice your stars while warm, not hot.

Citron

(Citrus medica)

In German, the lumpy, bumpy, yellow-green citron fruit is *Sukkade*, which may come from a Latin word meaning "juicy," as in "succulent," or from the Italian *zucchero*, "sugar."[175] The "socade" eaten by the Elizabethans was a marmaladelike citron conserve.[176] The German *Sukkade* usually refers to the citron's candied peel, since citrons are not good to eat fresh—they're more zest than flesh anyway. The word *Zitronat* really ought to mean "candied lemon peel" (lemon in German is *Zitrone*), but it is more often used to mean "candied citron peel." Another German word for the citron fruit is *Zitronatzitrone*, "candied lemon peel lemon," a very lemony word indeed for something that is not a lemon at all.

The citron was the first citrus fruit to be domesticated, probably in northeastern India, arriving in the Levant in time to be incorporated into the Old Testament *hag hassukôt*, "pilgrimage festival of booths."[177;178] Though the *esrog*, "citron," is chosen for its outward appearance, not its sweetness, it can be

175. *Merriam-Webster.com Dictionary*, s.v. "sugar," accessed January 25, 2023, https://www.merriam-webster.com/dictionary/sugar.

176. Mintz, *Sweetness and Power*, 124.

177. Alan Davidson, *The Oxford Companion to Food*. 3rd ed. (Oxford, England: Oxford University Press, 2014) 191.

178. Baruch A. Levine, "The Autumn Festival of Ingathering" in *The Oxford Companion to the Bible*, ed. Bruce M. Metzger and Michael Coogan, (New York: Oxford University Press, 1993), 228.

cooked and eaten after the festival to help with childbirth.[179] The name *Sukkot*, as this harvest festival is now known, is unrelated to *Sukkade*, but it's quite possible that the diasporic Jews' need for a good-looking esrog to wave around during Sukkot paved the citron peel's way into Stollen, Lebkuchen, and other quintessential German Christmas pastries.

Cloves

(Eugenia aromatica)

The Portuguese, Spanish, English, and Dutch were remarkable only in their extreme passion for the spices they couldn't grow in their home countries, not for the distances they traveled in order to obtain them. In *The Book of Spice*, John O'Connell opens his entry on cloves with the remarkable discovery of these hard, dried flower buds inside a Syrian ruin dating to 1720 BCE, a time when clove trees grew only in the Moluccas, thousands of miles across the sea.

The English *clove* comes from the French *clou*, meaning "nail," which is what a clove looks like. The German word *Nelke* ("little nail" in Old Saxon or a later dialect) can mean either a clove or a carnation. Carnations, which sometimes go by the name *clove pinks*, smell a little like cloves. Meanwhile, *Nelkenpfeffer* (carnation pepper) is one of the German names for allspice. (The other is *Piment*.)

---

179. Chana Weisberg, *Expecting Miracles: Finding Meaning and Spirituality in Pregnancy through Judaism* (Jerusalem: Urim Publications, 2004), 134.

Coriander
(*Coriandrum sativum*)

The coriander seed has none of the soapy-in-a-good-way taste of the cilantro leaf, though they're from the same plant. The Egyptians used both the leaves and the seeds, but northern Europeans have always been partial to the seeds, which they could keep all winter. A Central Asian native, coriander probably arrived in Europe with or just ahead of the Romans. Coriander, which gives Magenbrot and Aachener Printen the herby note other Lebkuchen lack, is known to ease digestion and cut flatulence.

Corn

One of maize's Italian names, *granturco*, "Turkish grain," reflects the roundabout route by which the first shipments arrived in Venice. Then again, calling something Turkish might simply have been a way of making it sound exotic, like the "turkeys" that started arriving on European tables around the same time as corn, the first leg appearing in Henry VIII's fist in the 1520s. But was corn completely unknown in the Old World before 1492? There's evidence to suggest that earlier explorers had already brought back word of it, and of the lands to the west. Acting on information from Portuguese sailors who had either seen the South American coast for themselves or had heard about it from West African sailors, the Portuguese King João II made theoretical claim to the lands now known as Brazil several years before they were officially "discovered."[180]

180. Krondl, *The Taste of Conquest*, 126–127.

Up in Scotland, the supposed ears of maize arching over a window in the South Aisle of Rosslyn Chapel were carved when both Christopher Columbus and King João were still in swaddling clothes. Popular theory holds that the chapel founder's grandfather, Henry St. Clair, Ninth Baron of Rosslyn, brought back corn from a voyage he made to the New World in the fourteenth century. Henry was a descendant of Rognvald the Mighty, Earl of Orkney, so it's conceivable that he was born with an urge to go "a-viking." Still, I find it unlikely that such an adventure, completed only fifty years before the invention of the printing press, would not have made it into the historical record. Besides, Henry would have had to sail much farther south than the old Viking haunts of Greenland and Newfoundland to find the gardens where corn was grown. Perhaps these carvings don't represent corn at all; one might even say the plants in question look a little like melegueta.

In North America, cornmeal, called Indian meal, was sweetened and steamed and eaten as pudding, something the early English colonists were a lot better at making than cake. Eventually, they got the hang of making cornmeal johnny-cakes, a mainstay of the Appalachian "Old Christmas," which was still celebrated on January 6 (Christmas Day according to the Julian calendar) well into the twentieth century. Like his comrade the Gingerbread Boy, Johnny-Cake was another unfortunate hero of the "fleeing food" tale.

My Jane Parker fruitcake friend, Vivette, hailed from Charente-Maritime on the west coast of France where, as a child, she used to pop corn on the glowing Yule log. She also baked a yellow cornmeal cake called *milla* on Christmas Eve, the handwritten recipe for which I now have in my own recipe file.

MILLA CAKE

Ingredients

1½ cups (234 grams) yellow cornmeal

½ cup (60 grams) flour

1 cup (198 grams) sugar

2½ cups (590 milliliters) *boiling* milk (Vivette has underlined
the word *boiling*)

2 eggs

½ cup (113 grams) butter, melted in a 9" by 9" baking pan
(so you won't have to grease it)

2 teaspoons brandy or rum

In a large bowl, mix the cornmeal, flour, and sugar. Pour the boiling milk over the mixture and stir it until smooth (no lumps). Add the eggs and melted butter and the brandy or rum.

Pour the batter into the pan.

Bake at 400 F (200 C) for forty-five minutes.

Serve your milla warm on Christmas Eve.

Cranberry

(Vaccinium macrocarpon)

I first made cranberry relish when I was six, the process overseen by my kindergarten teacher, who also gave me my first taste of figgy pudding. I didn't like either of them, but making and tasting foods I knew only from story and song was a thrilling experience.

Eastern North America is home to more than one species of cranberry, but it's the water-loving "large cranberry" that has been eaten for thousands of years. French writers traveling in eastern Canada in the seventeenth and early eighteenth centuries noted that the Huron and Cree ate them raw, as a "conserve," and put them in *pemmican*—small cakes of dried meat and fat that could be kept for years.[181] It's not known when, exactly, the colonists started eating cranberries, but by 1796, cranberry sauce was familiar enough to Americans that when Amelia Simmons exhorted her readers to serve it with turkey in her *American Cookery*, she didn't deem it necessary to include a recipe.[182]

In my elementary school, not a year went by without a reading of Wende and Harry Devlin's *Cranberry Thanksgiving, Cranberry Christmas*, and *Old Black Witch*. I don't remember the Devlins ever visiting in person, but I found out later that they'd lived just over the Watchung Mountains in Mountainside, New Jersey. The fun thing about the books was that there was always a recipe included. Cranberries and highbush blueberries, which figure importantly in the plots of all the books, grow wild in southern New Jersey's Pine Barrens, so when I found out that the Pine Barrens had once had their own resident witch, I immediately pictured her looking like the Old Black Witch, with a healthy dose of the Cranberry Grandmother thrown in.

---

181. Charlotte Erichsen-Brown, *Medicinal and Other Uses of North American Plants: A Historical Survey with Special Reference to the Eastern Indian Tribes* (Mineola, New York: Dover, 1979) 206.

182. More of a pamphlet than a book at forty-seven pages, *American Cookery* is acknowledged to be the very first American cookbook. Byrn, *American Cake*, 24; Susan Stamberg, "When Turkey Met Cranberries: a dinner date from the 1700's, November 18, 2022, https://www.npr.org/2022/11/18/1135751773/susan-stamberg-cranberry-relish-thanksgiving.

The widow Peggy Clevenger (c. 1777–1857), known as Old Mother Clevenger, was Hessian, so she may originally have been christened Margarethe. She lived in a log cabin near the "Hanover Tract," which I presume was not far from the Jersey Devil's old haunt of Hanover Furnace.[183] Along with cranberry cultivation, the Pine Barrens were a center of glass and iron production, and the word *furnace* appears in several of the old town names. The Elector of Hanover was one of those German princes who sold his troops to the British, so Peggy probably wasn't the only "Hessian" in the area.

As so often happens to old women living alone in the woods, Peggy was rumored to be a witch. She could turn herself into a lizard or a hare, depending on how the mood took her, and she kept a fortune of gold coins in a stocking. Peggy, who was reportedly eighty years old when she burned to death—Hansel and Gretel style—inside her cabin in 1857, would have spent at least the early part of her childhood back in Hanover or Hessen-Kassel, where she'd probably gotten an earful of the brutally cautionary fairy tales that would soon be made popular, in distilled form, by those most famous sons of Hessen, the Brothers Grimm.

According to the official account of her death, Peggy was not a witch but an opium addict who'd neglected to bank her fire. No gold coins were found in the ashes of the cabin. No cranberry bread recipe, either. The one below is another recipe from my friend Vivette's files. She wrote it for me on an index card many years ago. I don't know where the recipe ultimately came from.

---

183. A chimerical, winged monster, the Jersey Devil was the cursed thirteenth child of yet another witch, Mother Leeds.

CRANBERRY CAKE

Ingredients
¾ cup (168 grams) butter
1 cup (120 grams) flour
1 cup (198 grams) sugar
2 eggs, beaten
1 12-ounce bag (340 grams) fresh cranberries
½ cup (71 grams) walnuts, chopped fine

To Top
½ cup (99 grams) sugar

Melt the butter in the pan. Pour it into a large bowl, let it cool a little, and mix it well with the other ingredients. Spread the batter in the buttered pan, sprinkle with sugar, and bake at 325 F for fifty-five minutes or until a knife inserted in the center comes out clean (except for a little cranberry juice).

Cubeb

(Piper cubeba)

As you can tell by its Latin name, this dried berry, also called cubebs, is a "true" Asian pepper and was once as popular in Europe as its close cousin, *Piper nigrum.* Cubeb is one of those antique spices the Venetians acquired from Constantinople along with zedoary and galingale. Originally grown in Indonesia, the spice's name comes from Arabic *kababa*, which probably came from Sanskrit. A medieval Italian prescription advises the patient to drink cubeb in sweetened wine along with saffron, coriander, ground amber, pearls, gold, and other costly—and probably deadly—ingredients.[184] The taste of cubeb is usually described as a combination of black pepper and allspice, and in fact, in Polish, the word *kubaba* means "allspice." No wonder Columbus was confused.

Cumin
(Cuminum cyminum)

The ancient Egyptians grew the spindly cumin plant in their gardens, and in Graeco-Roman times, they spread the seeds under loaves of bread before they baked them as German bakers now spread aniseed under their Springerle.[185]

Galingale
(Alpinia galanga)

Here is another spice that, like cubebs and zedoary, would eventually be eclipsed in the West by pepper and ginger. Galingale (also spelled *galangal*) can refer to a number of species in the ginger family, some of which look like grasses, some of which look like hostas, though the rhizomes closely resemble gingerroot. The English name comes from a roundabout Arabicization of what might originally have been a Chinese word for ginger. In the Middle Ages, galingale, cinnamon, nutmeg, melegueta, ginger, lemon, and rosemary were steeped in sugared wine to make hippocras, a mulled wine that was enjoyed all year long, not just at Christmas. The herbs and spices were tied up in a conical bag known as a Hippocrates's sleeve, after the ancient Greek physician who was supposed to have invented it.

---

184. Krondl, *The Taste of Conquest*, 243.

185. Manniche, *An Ancient Egyptian Herbal*, 97.

Ginger

(Zingiber officinale)

Medieval Venetian merchants imported not just the ginger we're all familiar with today but also galingale, baladi, wild ginger, zedoary (a turmeric relative still used in Asian medicine), micchino via Mecca, and columbino via the port of Columbum (Kollam) in the South Indian kingdom of Travancore. All ginger family members do well in tropical climes, as witnessed by poet and *drabarni* (traditional Roma herbalist) Clarissa Simmens, who has cultivated *Zingiber officinale* at her home on Florida's Gulf Coast. She says it's the easiest thing she's ever grown, with the exception of cayenne peppers.

Early one spring, Clarissa cut up a gingerroot she'd bought from her local Asian grocery store and planted the pieces "eyes up" in a giant terracotta pot. Just before Halloween, when she was getting ready to make a pumpkin pie, she felt around in the soil and broke off a big piece of the root but left the newly established plant to keep growing. She was able to harvest more ginger for Thanksgiving and Christmas, and the following spring, her plant flowered, producing additional roots for one more year.

Clarissa also likes ginger for its warming properties and as a vehicle to bind with other healing herbs. She agrees with me that a flowering ginger stalk "looks like it has little fairies flitting around it," something those Venetian merchants hanging around the port in Alexandria never got to see.

Hazelnut

(Corylus avellana)

Stone Age Europeans didn't have to wait for the hazel tree to be carried up from the Mediterranean; Danish archaeologist P. V. Glob placed these shrubby trees on the Jutland peninsula by 7000 BCE, at which time hunter-gatherers in Britain were busy collecting the nuts, too. Finds of large pits of hazelnut shells suggest that the gathering of hazelnuts was a large-scale community activity, along the lines of a Hazelnut Festival. The Mesolithic Brits and Danes may even have elected a Hazelnut Queen, or at least a Chieftainess.

You may have noticed hazel trees growing in the backgrounds of medieval tapestries, usually with a shifty-looking red squirrel perched among the dark, crinkly leaves. Hazel trees form many of the hedgerows that run like green walls between roadways and cultivated fields, while a branch of the squiggly Contorta variety of *Corylus avellana* with its pale, drooping catkins looks like an avant-garde chandelier. Years ago, my German aunt hung such a branch in her picture window, where she keeps it decorated with her blue glass American witch ball and all the ornaments she doesn't feel like putting away after the Christmas tree comes down.[186]

---

186. Witch balls, which are always blue, were placed over the mouths of pitchers in Early American pantries, ostensibly to prevent witches from spoiling the milk inside.

Mace
(Myristica fragrans)

Mace is the aril or crimson webbing enclosing the hard seed inside the yellow fruit produced by the female nutmeg tree. Once it's removed from the seed, this lacy covering is dried in the sun and ground into a fluffy, rust-red powder that smells of fresh lemon peel to the dustier nutmeg's dried lemon peel.

Melegueta
(Aframomum melegueta)

One of the most fashionable spices of medieval European cuisine, where it was used like black pepper, melegueta, or "grains of Paradise," is still popular in its native West Africa, especially in Yoruba cooking. A member of the ginger family, it's the fruit, not the root, that is eaten. The name comes from *Malaguet*, an early Portuguese name for Mali.

Nutmeg
(Myristica fragrans)

For thousands of years, nutmeg trees grew only on the islands of a single archipelago in Indonesia's Banda Sea, and they can still only be grown in the tropics. So how did the New England state of Connecticut get the nickname "the Nutmeg state"? The prevailing theory is that traveling Yankee peddlers sold fake nutmegs whittled from clothespins. By this time, the real thing was being grown in the West Indies and was a lot cheaper than it had been when it was only grown in Indonesia. If you take into account the time it would take to carve a fake wooden nutmeg, a real nutmeg would have cost a lot less.

Those peddlers didn't only sell nutmegs; the real profits came from the little silver graters that came with them. Customers who acquired nutmegs without the grater, and without a demonstration, may have assumed that the nutmeg, like other tree nuts, had to be cracked. When the "nut" proved to be wood through and through, albeit a very fragrant wood, they may have thought they'd been cheated.

The nutmeg on Grenada's flag shows the nutmeg fruit in cross section, the red "nut" embedded in the yellow flesh.

Nutmeg has a reputation as an easily accessible alternative to cannabis, but you'd need to ingest a lot more than the sprinkling on your eggnog to feel any effects. Nutmeg is definitely a less-is-more kind of spice, at least to this twenty-first-century American's palate. I can't imagine how anyone could ever get enough of it down to get high. Before you try it at home, don't: too much nutmeg is toxic.

Pecan
(Carya illinoinensis)

"Illinois nuts" are a kind of hickory nut and have been cultivated in the American South since the eighteenth century. The pecan's name comes from an Algonquian word, possibly via Spanish. Americans can't agree on how to pronounce it.

Pine Nut
(Pinus pinea)

In English, a "pine nut" can be the fruit of the European stone pine, *Pinus pinea*, or of the shrubby American piñon pine, *Pinus edulis*, or of any variety of Asian pine, some of which, when eaten raw, can leave a metallic taste in the mouth for a few days, a condition known as pine mouth. The Italian recipes in this book call for the nuts known in Italian as *pinoli* but which Italian Americans insist on calling pignoli (*pin-YO-lee*) nuts. In Florentine dialect, a pine nut is a *pinocchio*, an interesting choice of name for everybody's favorite pine wood puppet, considering that *Pinocchio* author Carlo Collodi's father was a chef. Pine nuts, like acorns, were an important source of nutrition for Stone Age Europeans. In today's Italy, they're mostly used in pesto sauce and to top marzipan-based cakes and southern Italian cookies. They occur in Italian American Christmas cookies too. Pinocchio wouldn't be advised to eat any of these foods—cannibalism, you know.

Pignoli Cookies

Ingredients

1 egg white

1 cup (198 grams) sugar

1 cup (84 grams) blanched, ground almonds

1 batch homemade marzipan or 1 cup (about 300 grams) store-bought marzipan

Topping

¾ cup (105 grams) whole pine nuts

¼ cup (28 grams) powdered sugar

Beat the egg white with the sugar until stiff peaks form. Stir in the almonds and marzipan to make a sticky dough. Let sit one hour uncovered or until dry enough that you can scoop up a tablespoon-sized mound with a teaspoon.

Spread pine nuts over a plate and, using two teaspoons, drop mounds one at a time onto the pine nuts.

Pick up carefully and transfer, pine nut side up, to baking sheet.

Bake at 350 F (177 C) for fifteen to twenty minutes or until slightly golden.

Let cookies sit a few minutes on the sheet before moving them to a plate and dusting with powdered sugar.

Refrigerated, they'll stay crunchy on the outside, chewy on the inside for at least two weeks.

Makes forty-two cookies.

Rose

(Rosa damascena)

I buy my rose water the same place I buy my almonds, dates, and unsalted pistachios: at the Bhavani Cash & Carry in Greenbrook, New Jersey. But Europe's earliest marzipan makers had to get it all the way from Persia. The Arabic word *jūlab*, which is the source of the English word *julep*, as in "mint julep," comes from Persian *golāb*, "rose water."[187] Rose syrup is made from rose hips, but rose water, which is crystal clear, is distilled from the petals—lots and lots of petals. Ibn Sinna is sometimes credited with inventing rose water, but it had probably been around for a long time before he came along. The Persians added rose water to just about everything that had sugar in it, a practice the confectioners of the Abassid Caliphate quickly adopted and passed on to the Europeans.

Saffron

(Crocus sativus)

In her influential book *The Art of Cookery* (London, 1747), Hannah Glasse advises her readers to mix "a little canary" with orange flower water to color a marzipan hedgehog.[188] "Canary saffron," *Carthamus tinctorius*, or "safflower," was an affordable alternative to the precious threads of the saffron crocus. Saffron is often touted as the world's priciest spice, which it is, if you buy it in the store. Glasse, who moved around a lot with her financially insecure husband and five living children and who wrote *The Art of Cookery* to help make ends meet, probably never had her own patch of saffron crocuses, but many English cooks grew them in walled kitchen gardens.[189] Some towns, like Saffron Walden in Essex, grew saffron in large quantities to sell.

---

187. Encyclopedia Iranica, "GOLĀB," February 9, 2012, https://www.iranicaonline.org/articles/golab.

188. Historic Foodways, "A Marzipan Hedgehog," October 24, 2020, https://www.colonialwilliamsburg.org/learn/recipes/marzipan-hedgehog/.

189. Anne Willan, *Women in the Kitchen: Twelve Essential Cookbook Writers Who Defined the Way We Eat, from 1661 to Today* (New York: Scribner, 2020), 33.

In *The Old Magic of Christmas*, I included a recipe for the Swedish pastries Lussekatter that were actually shaped liked cats (or cat's heads, at least). The Goat, which is just the goat's head, and the Wagon Wheels below are traditional Swedish shapes. You don't need much saffron to color them; a pinch of saffron "threads," which are the stigma of the flower, will do.

Recipe

LUSSEKATTER

Ingredients

¼ cup (56 grams) butter plus a little more for greasing the bowl

½ cup (118 milliliters) milk

1 small pinch saffron threads

2¼ cups (270 grams) flour

¼ teaspoon cardamom

¼ cup (50 grams) sugar

One half of a .25-ounce package (3.5 grams) active dry yeast

1 egg

Topping

1 egg white, lightly beaten

2 tablespoons sugar

In a small pot, heat the butter and milk together just until the butter is melted. Turn off heat, crumble the saffron threads, and add them to the pot. Let sit.

In a large bowl, mix half a cup flour, cardamom, sugar, and yeast. Stir in milk mixture gradually, alternating with rest of flour. Stir in egg.

Knead the dough for ten minutes on a floured surface. Shape into a ball, place in a greased bowl, cover with a damp dish towel, and let rise in a warm place forty-five minutes.

Punch the dough down, cover with a towel, and let rest five minutes.

Pinch off a piece of dough a little larger than a golf ball. Roll it into a log and shape as in Figure 11a, the Goat. Make more logs to form Figure 11b, the Wagon Wheels.

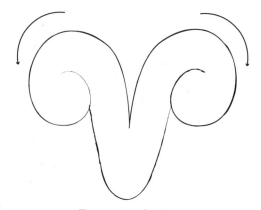

Figure 11a: the Goat

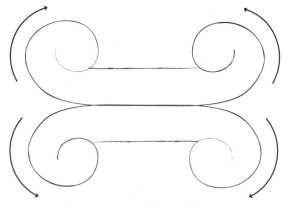

Figure 11b: the Wagon Wheels

Repeat with the rest of the dough, placing the buns on a baking sheet at least two inches apart. Cover with the towel and let rest ten minutes.

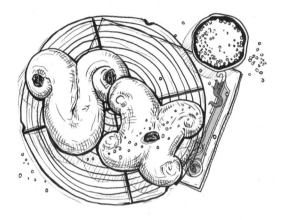

Brush the buns with the beaten egg white, sprinkle with sugar, and bake at 375 F for ten to fifteen minutes or until golden brown (they'll still be yellow on the inside).

Saunders

(Pterocarpus soyauxii)

The fifteenth-century panfortelike gyngerbrede dough mentioned in chapter 9 could be tinted yellow with saffron or red with *saunders*, a medieval English name for the powdered bark of this Indian tree.[190] Because it was used principally as incense, as it still is today, the *sandal* in *sandalwood* comes from the same ancient Indo-European root as *candle*, meaning "glowing." The name *sandalwood* refers to several species, but *saunders* denoted only the edible red sandalwood, *Pterocarpus soyauxii*.

---

190. A Dollop of History, "Medieval Gyngerbrede."

Star Anise
(Illicium verum)

Unrelated to aniseed, which is an herb, the yellow star anise fruit grows on a tall Asian tree. Both plants contain anethole, which is why they both taste like licorice, another East Asian tree. The star-shaped fruits contain star-shaped seedpods, one seed in each of the eight "points." Ground, the seeds are one of the spices in "Chinese five spice powder." Though some German bakers use the ground seeds, the pods are more often floated in mulled wine.

Sugar
(Saccharum officinarum)

Wild sugarcane was first domesticated in New Guinea about ten thousand years ago, Austronesian seafarers carrying it to the Philippines, Taiwan, and China, where ancient farmers fed *Saccharum sinese*, "Chinese sugar," to their pigs. The sturdiest species were used to build houses, while the softer canes were chewed.[191] It wasn't until sugarcane reached India around 400 BCE that this "honey reed," as Europe's First Crusaders would call it when they found it growing in Lebanon, was milked as a sweetener.[192]

The American kitchen might have a sack of white sugar, a box of powdered sugar, a box of brown sugar, and, if you're lucky, a jar of molasses, but there are many more varieties of

191. Willem H. Kampen, "Sugarcane History," LSU College of Agriculture, May 6, 2005, accessed July 10, 2022, https://www.lsuagcenter.com/portals /communications/publications/agmag/archive/2002/fall/sugarcane-history.

192. Mintz, *Sweetness and Power*, 28.

sugar, all made from the same species of this moisture-loving Asian grass.

In addition to cassonade, which is roughly equivalent to our brown sugar, there is the British baker's caster sugar, finer than granulated sugar but not as fine as powdered; sanding sugar, whose large, square crystals are dyed bright colors to sprinkle on top of cookies before they go in the oven; large-grained demerara sugar, which still contains some molasses; turbinado sugar, which is even less refined and whose mid-size crystals lend their crunch to Aachener Printen; and muscovado sugar, a dark, sandy sugar with a stronger taste than brown sugar. In the case of brown sugar, both dark and light, the molasses has been added back in, whereas in muscovado sugar, it was never taken out.[193] One of the most intriguing kinds of sugar I discovered in my research is the Haitian *rapadou*, a log of unrefined sugar wrapped in a banana leaf.[194]

I've yet to get my hands on rapadou (gifts can be sent to my publisher), but I now prefer the naturally amber brown demerara sugar to the colored sanding sugar I used to use at Christmastime. The first time I tried demerara sugar, it was on top of one of the mincemeat cookies my mother had baked for her then-one-hundred-year-old neighbor Austin.[195] Austin's English-born wife had recently died, and he had no one to make her signature Christmas cookies for him. Austin passed

---

193. Kelly Foster, "A Complete Visual Guide to 11 Different Kinds of Sugar," last updated, May 20, 2019, https://www.thekitchn.com/a-complete -visual-guide-to-sugar-ingredient-intelligence-213715.

194. Mintz, *Sweetness and Power*, xxii.

195. Austin, who is now 102, is also a Stollen connoisseur. Every December, he stocks up at the Aldi in Union, New Jersey, freezes the surplus, and eats a slice for breakfast every morning. He likes my mother's Stollen, but two years ago, he pronounced my Original Orange Cranberry Thanksgiving Stollen "a little dry."

the recipe on to my mother along with the dried mincemeat (which does indeed contain a little bit of beef) and the demerara sugar.

Mincemeat Cookies

Ingredients

4 ½ ounces (½ package) None Such or other brand condensed
    mincemeat

½ cup (113 grams) butter

¾ cup (150 grams) sugar

½ teaspoon vanilla extract

½ teaspoon rum extract

1 egg

1½ cups (180 grams) flour

½ teaspoon baking soda

¼ cup (55 grams) demerara sugar

Break up the mincemeat in a bowl. Set aside.

In another bowl, cream the butter and sugar. Add the extracts and beat in the egg.

Stir in the flour, baking soda, and mincemeat. Work into a smooth dough, roll into a log, wrap in plastic, and refrigerate at least one hour.

Spread the demerara sugar on a plate.

Slice the log into cookies with ¼-inch thickness and place each on the plate to pick up a coating of sugar on one side. Place them on the cookie sheet sugar side up and bake at 375 F (190 C) for eight to ten minutes.

Vanilla

(Vanilla planifolia)

The vanilla "bean" is the fruit of an orchid-bearing vine that wraps itself around other trees. Vanilla is native only to Central America where the flowers are pollinated exclusively by native hummingbirds and Melipona bees.[196] At the time the Spanish arrived in Mexico, the subjugated Totonac tribe were paying their tribute to the Aztecs in green vanilla pods.[197] (The wizened black beans you can buy in a jar are the dried pods.)

The method that is still used to pollinate the flowers today, in the absence of hummingbirds and Melipona bees, was devised by twelve-year-old Edmond Albius on the island of Réunion (formerly Bourbon) in the Indian Ocean.[198] It's not known who his father was, but Edmond was born into slavery in 1829 and sent to work at an estate belonging to Féréol Bellier Beaumont while still a child. Beaumont taught the young Edmond horticulture and referred to him as "a favorite child, always at my feet."[199] According to Beaumont, Edmond arrived at his pollination method, which employs two pointed sticks, a thumb, an index finger, and a delicate touch, all on his own.[200] Edmond

196. Nancy J. Hajeski, *National Geographic Complete Guide to Herbs and Spices* (Washington, DC: National Geographic Company, 2015), 230.

197. Bryan Quoc Le, PhD, "There's Nothing 'Vanilla' About Vanilla," October 20, 2018, https://medium.com/s/story/vanilla-a-legendary-flavor-6f5691cb6a0d.

198. Simran Sethi, "The Bittersweet Story of Vanilla," Smithsonian Magazine, April 3, 2017, https://www.smithsonianmag.com/science-nature/bittersweet-story -vanilla-180962757/.

199. Dr. Y, "Edmond Albius, the Slave who launched the Vanilla Industry," November 14, 2013, https://afrolegends.com/2013/11/14/Edmond-albius-the-slave-who -launched-the-vanilla-industry/.

200. Sethi, "The Bittersweet Story of Vanilla."

didn't gain his freedom until 1848 when France abolished slavery in its colonies, at which time he took the surname Albius, Latin for "white." Neither Edmond nor Beaumont prospered from Edmond's innovation, but Beaumont supported Edmond in court when he was accused of theft (as many former slaves were in the years after emancipation) and campaigned for his recognition by the horticulturists of the day.[201]

The following recipe, like most crescent-shaped cookies, is Viennese. To make the powdered vanilla sugar, slit a vanilla bean open lengthwise and leave it in the canister with your powdered sugar for one week to forever.

Recipe

VANILLEKIPFERL

Ingredients

2 cups (240 grams) flour

⅓ cup (66 grams) sugar

1¾ cups (147 grams) blanched, ground almonds

½ cup (113 grams) plus 6 tablespoons cold butter

1½ cups (169 grams) powdered vanilla sugar

In a large bowl, mix the flour, sugar, and almonds. Cut the butter in with two knives until the mixture looks like coarse crumbs. Use your hands to shape the dough into a ball. Wrap it tightly and refrigerate it for half an hour.

Take the dough out and roll it into balls a tablespoonful at a time. Roll each ball into a log and place it on a cookie sheet in a C shape, pinching the ends gently.

201. Euell A. Nielsen, "Edmond Albius (1829–1880)," September 13, 2020, https://www.blackpast.org/African-american-history/Edmond-albius-1829–1880/.

Bake at 350 F (177 C) for fifteen to twenty minutes or until very light golden.

Put the crescents on a plate and sprinkle with powdered sugar while still warm. Let them cool completely before storing. Makes about forty.

Zante Currant
(*Vitis vinifera*)

Zante currants are not to be confused with red or black currants, which are berries. Zante currants are dried Corinthian grapes, which were originally grown on the island of Zante in the Ionian Sea. Corinthian grapes were made into raisins thousands of years before other varieties of grapes.

I went through a lot of Zante currants back in the nineties when I was baking cakes for the Sunday Tea and Tours at the Museum of Early Trades and Crafts. Because they had to be imported, currants were a fairly expensive item in the Early American pantry. Because they were dried, they could be kept for long periods of time, which made them worth the money. The appearance of Zante currants in a tea cake marked a special occasion at any time of year but especially at Christmas, when there were no fresh fruits to be had. Zante currants, whose teeny tiny seeds are easily chewed, were easy to use, too. Before the advent of the Thompson seedless grape, other raisins had to be "stoned."

Conclusion
Back to the Black Land

Is it Christmas yet? No, not for another 1,400 years and 162 days, give or take. It's only the fifteenth century BCE, and it's July, not December. Today is the festival of Wepet Renpet, the ancient Egyptian New Year, when Sirius, the dog star, reappears in the morning sky after a seventy-day sojourn in the underworld, and the Nile overflows her banks to deliver the rich silt that makes the Black Land black. Rekhmire, the Vizier whose many duties included overseeing the baking of tiger nut cakes for the gods, passed on to the Field of Rushes himself a few years ago, and we've come to pay our respects. The mood is high here in the Theban necropolis—there's a lot of beer drinking going on—and I wouldn't want the old man's tomb to get overlooked.

To the Egyptians, the dog star was the goddess Sopdet who, by Rekhmire's time, was portrayed as a queen in a close-fitting linen garment, jeweled collar, and bulb-shaped crown topped by the five-pointed star of the underworld. Earlier farmers saw her as a cow with a bit of riverweed caught between her horns. Whatever shape she took, Sopdet embodied fertility, her appearance signaling the farmers to go out and plant the fields with barley, spelt, einkorn, and emmer wheat. But there's still time for all that: on Wepet Renpet, one puts one's work aside to feed and honor the dead.

Three and a half thousand years from now, the Theban necropolis will be a city of sand-scoured rock, but tonight it's a garden, the boughs of a fig tree shading the false door of Rekhmire's tomb. Lighting the first candle, we greet the Vizier's likeness on the panel above the narrow aperture cut into the granite "door." In the picture, Rekhmire sits before the sort of offering table his *ka*, or life force, is probably hoping we'll prepare for him. A ka is a ghost that can walk through walls, and false doors, so he'll be able to step out and enjoy the tiger nut cakes, raisins, loaves of lotus bread, and bowl of beer, flavored with coriander and honey, that we're serving him tonight.

We light a plain little candle so we can see what we're doing, but for Rekhmire, we've brought an enormous, cone-shaped candle, the tallow colored red with the juice of the alkanet root. As you can see from the blackened wick, it's already been burned a little, not by us but by the priests in the temple. We set the consecrated candle on its wooden stand beside the offering table and drape it in chains of persea, olive, and celery leaves, papyrus blossoms, lotus flowers, and bright red nightshade berries. When we light it, it looks like … well, I suppose it looks a little like a Christmas tree. See how the hieroglyphs carved in the stone dance in the light of the flame? The image of Rekhmire appears to lean forward in his chair, reaching for the tiger nut cake at the top of the heap.

Eat well, Rekhmire, and rest in peace.

Appendix

Paper Angel Stencils

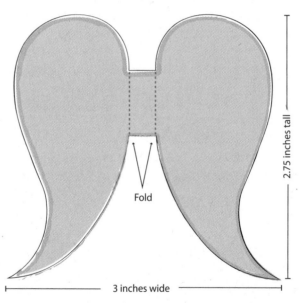

2.75 inches tall

Fold

3 inches wide

Wing Stencil

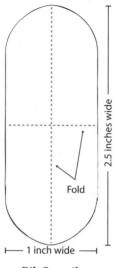

2.5 inches wide

Fold

1 inch wide

Bib Stencil

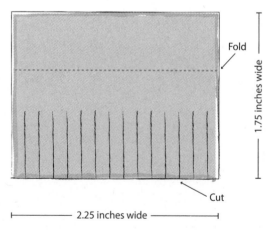

Fold

1.75 inches wide

Cut

2.25 inches wide

Fringed Pieces Stencil (need 3 of these)

Marzipan Coats of Arms Stencils

Basic Shield

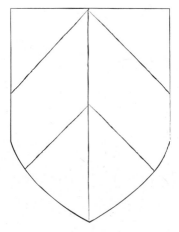

Striped Shield

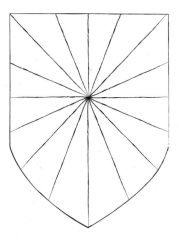

Scoring the Shield

Sun Shield   **Moon Shield**

Bibliography

Books

Berolzheimer, Ruth, ed. *The American Woman's Cook Book.* New York: Garden City Publishing Company, 1940.

Byrn, Anne. *American Cake: From Colonial Gingerbread to Classic Layer, the Stories and Recipes behind More Than 125 of Our Best-Loved Cakes from Past to Present.* New York: Rodale, 2016.

Davidson, Alan. *The Oxford Companion to Food.* 3rd ed. Oxford, England: Oxford University Press, 2014.

dePaola, Tomie. *The Legend of Old Befana.* New York: Houghton Mifflin Harcourt Publishing Company, 1980.

Dooley, Brendan. *A Companion to Astrology in the Renaissance.* Boston: Brill, 2014.

Erbrich, Guido, Rafael Ledschbor, Anja Pohontsch, and Mirko Pohontsch. *Wo Krabat das Zaubern lernte: Unterwegs in sorbischen Oberlausitz.* Bautzen, Germany: Domowina-Verlag, 2010.

Erichsen-Brown, Charlotte. *Medicinal and Other Uses of North American Plants: A Historical Survey with Special Reference to the Eastern Indian Tribes.* Mineola, NY: Dover, 1979.

Fertig, Theresa Kryst. *Christmas in the Netherlands*. Chicago: World Book-Childcraft International, 1981.

Glob, P. V., *Denmark: An Archaeological History from the Stone Age to the Vikings*. Translated from the Danish by Joan Bulman. Ithaca, NY: Cornell University Press, 1971.

Grimm, Jacob. *Teutonic Mythology, Volumes I–III*. Translated by James Steven Stallybrass. London: George Bell and Sons, 1883. Republished by Dover Books, 2004.

Grüger, Heribert und Johannes. *Die Weihnachtsliederfiebel: Laterne-, Weihnachts- und Winterlieder*. Düsseldorf: Patmos, 2001.

Guiley, Rosemary Ellen. *Encyclopedia of Witches and Witchcraft*. 2nd ed. New York: Checkmark Books, 1999.

Hajeski, Nancy J. *National Geographic Complete Guide to Herbs and Spices*. Washington, DC: National Geographic Company, 2015.

Hale, Sarah Josepha. *Early American Cookery: "The Good Housekeeper," 1841*. Mineola, NY: Dover Publications, 1996.

Homer. *The Odyssey*. Translated by Robert Fagles. New York: Viking, 1996.

Hutton, Ronald. *The Stations of the Sun*. Oxford: Oxford University Press, 1996.

Jacobson, Dawn. *Chinoiserie*. London: Phaidon, 1993.

Jerman, Tom A. *Santa Claus Worldwide: A History of St. Nicholas and Other Holiday Gift-Bringers*. Jefferson, NC: McFarland, 2020.

Krondl, Michael. *The Taste of Conquest: The Rise and Fall of the Three Great Cities of Spice.* New York: Ballantine Books, 2007.

Krusendorfer Keksteller: bewählte Rezepte, gesammelt rund um den Kirchturm.

Levine, Baruch A. "The Autumn Pilgrimage Festival of Ingathering." In *The Oxford Companion to the Bible*, edited by Bruce M. Metzger and Michael D. Coogan, 227–228. New York: Oxford University Press, 1993.

Longone, Janice (Jan) Bluestein. "Introduction to the Dover Edition." In *Early American Cookery: "The Good House-keeper," 1841*, by Sarah Josepha Hale, v–x. Mineola, NY: Dover Publications, 1996.

Manniche, Lisa. *An Ancient Egyptian Herbal.* Austin, Texas: University of Texas Press, 1989.

Mayers, Robert A. *Searching for Yankee Doodle: Washington's Soldiers in the American Revolution.* Staunton, Virginia: American History Press, 2016.

McNeill, F. Marian. *Hallowe'en: Its Origins, Rites and Ceremonies in the Scottish Tradition.* Edinburgh: The Albyn Press, no year.

Metzger, Christine, ed. *Culinaria Germany.* Cologne, Germany: Könemann Verlag, 1999.

Mintz, Sidney W. *Sweetness and Power: The Place of Sugar in Modern History.* New York: Penguin Books, 1985.

Moran, Rena. *Christmas in Ireland.* Chicago: World Book, 1985.

Morris, Jan. *Venice.* Third revised edition. London: Faber and Faber, 1993.

O'Connell, John. *The Book of Spice: From Anise to Zedoary.* New York: Pegasus Books, 2016.

Oetker, Dr. August. *Backen macht Freude.* Bielefeld, Germany: Ceres Verlag, 1952.

Palmer, Alan. *The Baltic: A New History of the Region and its People.* New York: Overlook Press, 2005.

Piras, Claudia. *Culinaria Italy: Pasta, Pesto, Passion.* Germany: H. F. Ullmann, 2004.

Poitras, Geoffrey. *Variation of Equity Securities: History, Theory, and Application.* Danvers, Massachusetts: World Science Publishing Company, 2011.

Raedisch, Linda. "Deep in the Wooded Glens: An Armchair Herbalist's Tour of Circe's House and Garden." In *Llewellyn's 2018 Herbal Almanac*, 269–277. Woodbury, Minnesota: Llewellyn, 2017.

Raedisch, Linda. *Night of the Witches: Folklore, Traditions, and Recipes for Celebrating Walpurgis Night.* Woodbury, Minnesota: Llewellyn, 2011.

Raedisch, Linda. *The Old Magic of Christmas: Yuletide Traditions for the Darkest Days of the Year.* Woodbury, Minnesota: Llewellyn, 2013.

Raedisch, Linda. "The Old Ways: Beer, Bread, and Candle." In *Llewellyn's 2014 Sabbats Almanac*, 247–250. Woodbury, Minnesota: Llewellyn, 2013.

Reich, Lilly Joss. *The Viennese Pastry Cookbook.* New York: Macmillan, 1970.

Ross, Corinne. *Christmas in Italy.* Chicago: World Book Encyclopedia, 1978.

Russell, Mrs. Malinda. *Domestic Cookbook: Containing a Careful Selection of Useful Receipts for the Kitchen.* Paw Paw, Michigan: Published by the author, 1866. https://www.google.com/books/edition/A_DomesticCook_Book/jtKETYEMepAC?hl=en&gbpv=1. Accessed November 6, 2022.

Steves, Rick, and Valerie Griffith. *Rick Steves' European Christmas.* Emeryville, California: Avalon Travel Publishing, 2005.

Thompson, Martha Wiberg, editor. *Superbly Swedish: Recipes and Traditions.* Iowa City, Iowa: Penfield Press, 1983.

Webster's New Twentieth Century Dictionary, Unabridged. Second Edition. World Publishing Company, 1960.

Weisberg, Chana. *Expecting Miracles: Finding Meaning and Spirituality in Pregnancy through Judaism.* Jerusalem: Urim Publications, 2004.

Wilkerson, Charmaine. *Black Cake: A Novel.* New York: Ballantine Books, 2022.

Willan, Anne. *Women in the Kitchen: Twelve Essential Cookbook Writers Who Defined the Way We Eat, from 1661 to Today.* New York: Scribner, 2020.

Other

Afro-Europe International Blog. "Suriname abolishes Sinterklaas (and Black Pete) again." December 14, 2011. https://afroeurope.blogspot.com/2011/12/suriname-abolishes-sinterklaas-and.html.

Anand, Pranav. "Anand/Vamosi Wedding." What's Happening at Santa Cruz? September 24, 2007. https://whascling.sites .ucsc.edu/2007/09/.

Auer, Kathrin. "Orangeat und Zitronat selber machen." Mein Schöner Garten. Accessed January 27, 2023. https://www .mein-schoener-garten.de/lifestyle/essen-trinken/rezepte /orangeat-zitronat-selber-machen-40027.

Avey, Tori. "The History of Gingerbread." PBS. December 20, 2013. https://www.pbs.org/food/the-history-of-ginger bread/history-gingerbread/.

Bäckerei Gnauck. "The History of the Christ Stollen from Dresden." Accessed January 24, 2023. https://www.stollen -online.de/dresdnerstollen/geschichte-eng.htm.

The Bahlsen Family. "History." Accessed November 20, 2022. https://www.thebahlsenfamily.com/int/company/about -us/history/.

"The Baker Arent Oostward and His Wife, Catharina Keizer-swaard, Jan Havicksz. Steen, 1658." Rijksmuseum. Accessed January 25, 2023. https://www.rijksmuseum.nl/en /collection/SK-A-390.

Bannemann, Ingolf. "Unterwegs mit Yared Dibaba: Weihnachten auf der Hallig." Accessed January 27, 2023. https://www.youtube.com/watch?v=D50psr7UjEI.

Bearden-White, Christina. "Gustav Goelitz." Immigrant Entrepreneurship. Last updated August 22, 2018. https:// www.immigrantentrepreneurship.org/entries/gustav -goelitz/.

Blitz, Matt. "The History of Peeps." Food and Wine. Last updated May 24, 2017. https://www.foodandwine.com /news/history-peeps.

Bowersox, Jeff. "St. Maurice in Magdeburg (CA. 1240)." Black Central Europe. Accessed June 3, 2022. https://blackcentral europe.com/sources/1000-1500/st-maurice-in-magdeburg -ca-1240/.

Britannica. "Dinanderie." Accessed September 21, 2022. https://www.britannica.com/art/dinanderie.

Bukechi. "Thorner Kathrinchen—Seit Jahrhunderten geb-acken." December 26, 2021. https://bukechi.com/thorner -kathrinchen/.

Burton, Monica, Osayi Endolyn, and Toni Tipton-Martin. "The Legacy of Malinda Russell, the First African-Ameri-can Cookbook Author." February 23, 2021. https://www .eater.com/22262716/malinda-russell-author-a-domestic -cookbook.

Cacaoweb. "Cocoa Balls." Accessed June 17, 2022. https:// cacaoweb.net/cocoa-balls.html.

Callas, John. "Montecchi and Capalletti." Shakespeare Elec-tronic Conference, Volume 4, Number 408. July 2, 1993. https://shaksper.net/archive/1993/89-july/1318-montecchi -and-cappelletti.

Caserta Royal Palace and Park, Italy. "The Benevento Witches." Accessed January 24, 2023. https://visitworld heritage.com/en/eu/the-benevento-witches/6453590a -ff50-4a3a-8fe8-0a9a797b7b4e.

"Cattern Cakes for St. Catherine's Day." Bread, Cakes and Ale. November 21, 2016. https://breadcakesandale.com /2016/11/21/cattern-cakes-for-st-catherines-day/.

Chandler, Graham. "Sugar, Please." Aramco World Volume 63 Number 4. July/August 2012. https://archive.aramcoworld .com/issue/201204/sugar.please.htm.

ChefKoch. "Königsberger Marzipan aus Urgrossmutters Rezeptbuch." Accessed April 25, 2022. https://www .chefkoch.de/rezepte/1593571266648304/Koenigsberger -Marzipan-aus-Urgrossmutters-Rezeptbuch.html.

The Church of England. "The Twenty-Fifth Sunday after Trinity." Accessed January 25, 2023. https://www.church ofengland.org/prayer-and-worship/worship-texts-and -resources/book-common-prayer/collects-epistles -and-gospels-70.

Ciao Italia. "Fruitcake from Siena/Panforte di Siena." Accessed January 25, 2023. https://www.ciaoitalia.com /recipes/fruitcake-from-siena-panforte-di-siena.

Claxton Fruitcake. "The Claxton Story...It's All About Family!" Accessed June 14, 2022. https://claxtonfruitcake.com /about-us.

Dan. "Dante and Shakespeare: A Tale of Montagues and Capulets." November 17, 2013. https://secretsofinferno .wordpress.com/2013/11/17/dante-and-shakespeare-a -tale-of-montagues-and-capulets/.

Dewey's Bakery. "The Dewey's Bakery Story." Accessed November 6, 2022. https://deweys.com/pages/our-history.

A Dollop of History. "Frumenty, a Medieval Wheat Porridge." March 15, 2020. https://historydollop.com/2020/03/15/frumenty-a-medieval-wheat-porridge/.

A Dollop of History. "Medieval Gyngerbrede." December 11, 2018. https://historydollop.com/2018/12/11/medieval-gyngerbrede/.

Doyle, James. "The Drinking Cup of a Classic Maya Noble." September 25, 2014. Metropolitan Museum of Art. https://www.metmuseum.org/blogs/now-at-the-met/2014/maya-drinking-cup.

Dresdner Stollen Verband e.V. "Dresdner Christstollen." Accessed February 18, 2022. https://www.dresdnerstollen.com/de/.

Eamon, William. "Renaissance Astrology and the Vagaries of the Markets." November 27, 2011. https://williameamon.com/renaissance-astrology-and-the-vagaries-of-markets/.

Eigeland, Tor. "Arabs, Almonds, Sugar, and Toledo." Aramco World Volume 47, Number 3. April/June 1996. https://archive.aramcoworld.com/issue/199603/arabs.almonds.sugar.and.toledo.htm.

Encyclopedia Iranica. "GOLĀB." February 9, 2012. https://www.iranicaonline.org/articles/golab.

"English Ginger Biscuits—Cornish Fairings." Accessed June 7, 2022. https://recipesformen.com/cornish-fairings-english-ginger-biscuits.

Erasmi & Carstens GmbH. "Lübeck Marzipan." Accessed January 25, 2023. https://carstens-marzipan.de/en/luebecker-marzipan/index.html.

"Evernia prunastri." Accessed January 28, 2023. https://scratchpad.fandom.com/wiki/Evernia_prunastri.

Evangelisch-Lutherische Kirchengemeinde Krusendorf. "Ehemalige St. Katharinenkirche Jellenbek." Accessed January 25, 2023. https://www.kirchengemeinde-krusendorf.de/ehemalige-st-katharinenkirche-jellenbek.

Foster, Kelly. "A Complete Visual Guide to 11 Different Kinds of Sugar." Last updated May 30, 2019. https://www.thekitchn.com/a-complete-visual-guide-to-sugar-ingredient-intelligence-213715.

Gershon, Livia. "The Invention of Dessert." JSTOR Daily. August 23, 2019. https://daily.jstor.org/the-invention-of-dessert/.

Geschenke 2015. "The Devil's Earwax: A Cincinnati Candy Invented for Christmas, Not Halloween." November 2, 2021. https://dannwoellertthefoodetymologist.wordpress.com/2021/11/02/the-devils-earwax-a-cincinnati-german-candy-invented-for-christmas-not-halloween/.

Gottlieb, Laura. "The History of Honey Cake." The Nosher. September 1, 2020. https://www.myjewishlearning.com/the-nosher/the-history-of-honey-cake/.

Greenwalt, Phill. "The German Principalities that Contributed Soldiers." Emerging Revolutionary War Era. October 20, 2020. https://emergingrevolutionarywar.org/2020/10/20/the-german-principalities-that-contributed-soldiers/.

Helvetic Kitchen. "Magenbrot." Accessed March 12, 2022. https://www.helvetickitchen.com/recipes/magenbrot?rq=magenbrot.

Herrnhut. "Herrnhuter Sterne: The origin of the Christmas stars." Accessed January 25, 2023. https://www.herrnhuter -sterne.de/en/.

Heyl, Stephanie. "Stadt Nürnberg." Accessed September 21, 2022. Haus der Bayerische Geschichte. https://www.hdbg .eu/gemeinden/index.php/detail?rschl=9564000.

Hindustan Times. "Excerpt: *The Nutmeg's Curse* by Amitav Ghosh." October 9, 2021. http://www.hindustantimes .com/books/excerpt-the-nutmeg-s-curse-by-amitav -ghosh-101633692933273.html.

Historic Foodways. "A Marzipan Hedgehog." October 24, 2020. https://www.colonialwilliamsburg.org/learn/recipes /marzipan-hedgehog/.

Holly Trail. "Old-Style Polish Gingerbread Cookies ("Pier-niczki Staropolskie")." December 27, 2017. https://holly trail.com/2017/12/27/old-style-polish-gingerbread -cookies-pierniczki-staropolskie/.

Hoyerswerda.de. "Das war der Weihnachtsmarkt." December 17, 2018. https://www.hoyerswerda.de/2018/12/17 /das-war-der-weihnachtsmarkt/.

Images of Venice. "Teriaca—The Divine Potion." Accessed May 29, 2022. https://imagesofvenice.com/teriaca-the -divine-potion/.

Into the Cookie Jar. "Best Ever Cornish Fairings Recipe." Accessed June 7, 2022. https://www.intothecookiejar.com /cornish-fairings-recipe.

Isnaeni, Hendri F. "The VOC Genocide." Histori Bersama. April 5, 2010. http://historibersama.com/the-voc-genocide -historia/.

Jamaican Cookery. "How to Make Jamaican Chocolate Ball." November 15, 2016. https://www.jamaicancookery.com /2016/11/how-to-make-jamaican-chocolate-ball.html.

Jane Parker. "Frequently Asked Questions." Accessed January 25, 2023. https://janeparker.com/pages/faqs.

Jewish Virtual Library. "Nuremberg." Accessed September 21, 2022. https://www.jewishvirtuallibrary.org/nuremberg.

Jewish Virtual Library. "Virtual Jewish World: Cologne, Germany." Accessed September 21, 2022. https://www .jewishvirtuallibrary.org/cologne-germany-virtual-jewish -history-tour.

Kampen, Willem H. "Sugarcane History." LSU College of Agriculture. May 6, 2005. https://www.lsuagcenter.com /portals/communications/publications/agmag/archive /2002/fall/sugarcane-history.

Katz, Jonathan. "Gingerbread Cake." Flavors of Diaspora. January 16, 2019. https://flavorsofdiaspora.com/category /elite-dishes/.

Kayal, Michele. "Steinhart, duftend, lecker: Kulturgut Aachener Printen." December 6, 2019. https://www .nationalgeographic.de/geschichte-und-kultur/2019/12 /steinhart-duftend-lecker-kulturgut-aachener-printen.

Kerlen-Gramsch, Juliane. "Nürnberger Leckerei." *Landlust* November/Dezember 2013, 124–129.

"Knisternde Himmelsboten." Bayerische Staatszeitung. December 19, 2016. https://www.bayerische-staatszeitung .de/staatszeitung/kultur/detailansicht-kultur/artikel /knisternde-himmelsboten.html#topPosition.

Krüger, Sönke. "Gingerbread drama: The culinary heritage of the Germans is threatened." Welt. December 7, 2018. https://www.welt.de/iconist/essen-und-trinken/article 185097354/Pfefferkuchendrama-Das-kulinarische -Erbe-der-Deutschen-ist-bedroht.html.

Küchen Götter. "Klassische Aachener Printen." Accessed March 9, 2022. https://www.kuechengoetter.de/rezepte /klassische-aachener-printen-197.

Küchentraum & Purzelbaum. "Thorner Kathrinchen." November 25, 2018. https://www.kuechentraumundpurzel baum.de/thorner-kathrinchen/.

Kulinarisches Erbe der Schweiz. "Magenbrot, Pains á l'esto-mac." Accessed January 25, 2023. https://www.patrimoine culinaire.ch/Produit/Magenbrot-Pains-a-lestomac/377.

Lanari, Massimo. "The History of Torrone, an Italian Christ-mas Dessert." November 5, 2020. https://www .lacucinaitaliana.com/italian-food/italian-dishes/the -history-of-torrone-an-italian-christmas-dessert.

Laudan, Rachel. "Crossroads and Diaspora: A Thousand Years of Islamic Cuisines." Aramco World Volume 65 No. 6. November/December 2014. https://archive.aramcoworld .com/issue/201406/crossroads.and.diasporas.a.thousand .years.of.islamic.cuisines.htm.

Lausitzer Küche. "Vogelhochzeit (Ptači kwas/Ptaškowa swa-jźba)." Accessed January 25, 2023. https://dolneluzyce .pl/de/lausitzer-kueche/#:~:text=Vogelhochzeit%20 (Pta%C4%8Di%20kwas%20%2F%20Pta%C5%A1kowa%20 swaj%C5%Baba)&text=Am%20Tag%20der%20Vogel hochzeit%20beschenkt,im%20Winter%20flei%C3%9Fig%20 gef%C3%Bcttert%20haben.

Le, Bryan Quoc, PhD. "There's Nothing 'Vanilla' About Vanilla." October 20, 2018. https://medium.com/s/story /vanilla-a-legendary-flavor-6f5691cb6a0d.

Lindsy, Deb. "Trinidad Black Cake." The Washington Post. November 23, 2014. https://www.washingtonpost.com /recipes/trinidad-black-cake-/14387/.

Lodder, Karen. "What Is a Bunter Teller? A Plate of Cookies for Everyone!" German Girl in America. December 12, 2016. https://germangirlinamerica.com/what-is-a-bunter -teller/#:~:text=Bunter%20Teller%20translates%20as%20 %E2%80%9Ccolorful,that%20is%20given%20at%20 Christmas.

Lodder, Karen. "What Is a Rauschgoldengel? The Legend of the Golden Angel." German Girl in America. December 6, 2018. https://germangirlinamerica.com/what-is-a-rausch goldengel/.

London Eats. "Pulsnitzer Pfefferkuchen." December 24, 2020. https://londoneats.wordpress.com/2020/12/24/6 -pulsnitzer-pfefferkuchen/.

Lühr, Michaela. "Hallig Knerken—Rezept für die Seefahrer Kekse!" Last updated October 18, 2022. https://herzelieb .de/hallig-knerken-rezept-kekse-nordfriesland/.

Maria. "How to Make Nankhatai Recipe." Flavors of Mumbai. October 1, 2018. http://www.flavorsofmumbai.com/how -to-make-nankhatai-recipe/.

McGill University Office for Science and Society. "Of Mummies, Pigments and Pretzels." Accessed September 21, 2022. https://www.mcgill.ca/oss/article/history -technology/mummies-pigments-and-pretzels.

Merriam-Webster. "Sugar." Accessed January 25, 2023. https://www.merriam-webster.com/dictionary/sugar.

Metro Creative. "The story behind Jordan almonds." Richmond Times-Dispatch. June 29, 2014. https://richmond .com/the-story-behind-jordan-almonds/article_00c20dfa -fd5c-11e3-8165-001a4bcf6878.html.

Metropolitan Museum of Art. "Birth Tray (Desco da Parto) with the Triumph of Chastity (recto) and Naked Boys with Poppy Pods (verso) c. 1450–60." Accessed January 24, 2023. https://www.metmuseum.org/art/collection/search /479708.

Moshenska, G., (2017) Esoteric Egyptology, Seed Science and the Myth of the Mummy Wheat. *Open Library of Humanities*, 3(1): 1 pp. 1-42, DOI: February 16, 2017. https://olh .openlibhums.org/article/id/4430/.

Musacchio, Jacqueline Marie. "The Medici-Tornaburi *Desco da Parto* in Context." *Metropolitan Museum Journal*, Volume 33 (1998) 137-151. *JSTOR*, https://www.journals.u chicago.edu/doi/10.2307/1513010.

Museum of Food and Drink. "Fanny Steward." Accessed January 25, 2023. https://legacyquiltproject.mofad.org/quilt /fanny-steward/.

Museum of the American Revolution. "Christopher Ludwick's Cookie Board." Accessed June 26, 2022. https:// www.amrevmuseum.org/collection/Christopher-ludwick -s-cookie-board.

Musgrave, Christian. "Black Hessians." Black Central Europe. Accessed June 16, 2022. https://blackcentraleurope.com /biographies/black-hessians-christian-musgrave/.

Muzeum Piernika. "History." Accessed May 15, 2022. https:// muzeumpiernika.pl/en/.

Naparima Cookbook. "Trinidad Black Cake (With Alcohol)." December 18, 2011. https://naparimacookbook.com /Trinidad-black-cake-with-alcohol/.

Niederegger. "History of Marzipan." Accessed January 25, 2023. https://www.niederegger.de/en/marzipan/history -of-marzipan/.

Nielsen, Euell A. "Edmond Albius (1829–1880)." Blackpast. September 13, 2020. https://www.blackpast.org/African -american-history/Edmond-albius-1829-1880/.

O'Neill, Molly. "A 19th-Century Ghost Awakens to Redefine 'Soul.'" New York Times. November 21, 2007. http://www .nytimes.com/2007/11/21/dining/21cook.html.

Online Etymology Dictionary. "Candy." Accessed January 25, 2023. https://www.etymonline.com/word/candy.

Osman, Nadia. "What's Different about Coptic Christmas?" Middle East Eye. January 7, 2020. https://www.middleeast eye.net/discover/what-different-about-coptic-christmas.

PBS. "Hessians." *Liberty! The American Revolution.* Accessed October 6, 2022. https://www.pbs.org/ktca/liberty/popup _hessians.html.

Palma, Jennifer. "The Witches of Venice." University of Miami. Accessed January 29, 2023. https://news.miami.edu/stories /2017/10/witches-of-venice.html. 2017.

Pasticceria Costantini. "Peverino." Accessed April 25, 2022. www.pasticceriacostantini.com/product/peverino.

Pettitt, Alena Kate. "Gingerbread Husbands: An Elizabethan All Hallow's Eve Recipe." The Darling Academy. October

28, 2020. https://www.thedarlingacademy.com/articles
/gingerbread-husbands-a-vintage-all-hallows-eve-recipe/.

Pozza, Cristina. "Traditional Veronese Christmas Cakes." Guide Verona-Italy. December 24, 2021. http://www.guide verona.net/traditional-veronese-christmas-cakes/.

Pulsnitzer Lebkuchen Fabrik GmbH. "Pulsnitz die Pfefferkuchen Stadt." Accessed January 25, 2023. https://www .pulsnitzer-lebkuchen.de/ueber_uns/index.php?id=29.

Pulsnitzer Lebkuchen Fabrik GmbH. "Von Anis bis Zitronat." Accessed January 25, 2023. https://www.pulsnitzer -lebkuchen.de/ueber_uns/index.php?id=25.

Rich, Viktoria Greenboim. "The 'Amber Elites' in Ancient Kaliningrad Went to Eternity With Their Horses." Haaretz/ Archaeology. December 28, 2021. https://www.haaretz .com/archaeology/2021-12-28/ty-article/the-amber-elites -in-ancient-kaliningrad-went-to-eternity-with-their -horses/0000017f-dc08-d3ff-a7ff-fda861510000.

Rolek, Barbara. "The History of Gingerbread." The Spruce Eats. Last updated November 10, 2019. https://www.the spruceeats.com/the-history-of-gingerbread-1135954#:~: text=The%20first%20gingerbread%20man%20is,became %20a%20token%20of%20love.

Rolek, Barbara. "Polish Gingerbread Cookies (Pierniczki)." The Spruce Eats. Last updated April 12, 2022. https://www .thespruceeats.com/polish-gingerbread-cookies-pierniczki -recipe-1136960.

Rushing, Erin. "Holiday Cooking with Hannah Glasse." Unbound Smithsonian Library and Archives. December 14, 2021. https://blog.library.si.edu/blog/2021/12/14 /holiday-cooking-with-hannah-glasse/#.Y9P-KnbMLIV.

St. Onge, Danielle. "Pandoro (Verona Christmas Cake)." The
Spruce Eats. August 24, 2021. https://www.thespruceeats
.com/pandoro-classic-christmas-cake-verona-recipe
-4120205.

Schaller, Dr. Wendy. "Jan Steen, The Feast of St. Nicholas."
Khan Academy. Accessed September 28, 2022. https://
www.khanacademy.org/humanities/renaissance
-reformation/baroque-art1/holland/a/jan-steen-feast-of
-st-nicholas.

Schenawolf, Harry. "Black Hessians: German Troops Enlisted
Former African American Slaves in the American Revolution." April 15, 2021. https://www.revolutionarywarjournal
.com/black-hessians-german-troops-enlisted-former
-african-american-slaves-in-the-american-revolution/.

Schönleben, Martin. "Gebackene Vögelchen—25 Januar Sankt
Pauli Bekehrung." January 19, 2013. https://cafe
schoenleben.de/gebackene-vogelchen-25-januar-sankt
-pauli-bekehrung/.

Sethi, Simran. "The Bittersweet Story of Vanilla." Smithsonian
Magazine. April 3, 2017. https://www.smithsonianmag
.com/science-nature/bittersweet-story-vanilla-180962757/.

Shattuck, Gary. "George Washington's 'Baker Master.'" Journal
of the American Revolution. May 27, 2015. https://all
thingsliberty.com/2015/05/George-washingtons-baker
-master/.

Shaw, Sumit Osmand, and Anu Radha. "A Little Poland in
India (English)—The Complete Documentary." Aakaar-
Films. Accessed January 27, 2023. https://www.youtube
.com/watch?v=rIPq-8RZxxM.

"Stadt Nürnberg—Haus der Bayerische Gescichte." Accessed May 22, 2022. https://hdbg.eu/gemeinden/index.php /detail?schl=9564000.

Stamberg, Susan. "When turkey met cranberries: a dinner date from the 1700s." November 18, 2022. https://www .npr.org/2022/11/18/1135751773/susan-stamberg -cranberry-relish-thanksgiving.

Sula, Mike. "Omnivorous: The Cookbook Queen: The story of a lost Chicago culinary empire and its guiding force, Ruth Berolzheimer." September 11, 2008. https://chicagoreader .com/food-drink/omnivorous-the-cookbook-queen/.

Thermomix Rezeptwelt. "Knerken: Seefahrer Gebäck von der Hallig." November 16, 2014. https://www.rezeptwelt.de /backen-suess-rezepte/knerken-seefahrer-gebaeck -von-der-hallig/rhehtv82-a88b5-175680-cfcd2-4p5mwdim.

Throughline. "Zombies." NPR. October 31, 2019. npr.org /2019/10/30/774809210/.

Tiwari, Anuj. "How an Indian Maharajah Helped Save the Lives of Thousands of Polish People During World War II." September 11, 2021. https://www.indiatimes.com/trending /social-relevance/maharaja-jam-saheb-digvijaysinhji-and -world-war-ii-polish-refugees-story-549242.html.

Turner, Jack. "The Spice That Built Venice." Smithsonian Magazine. November 2, 2015. https://www.smithsonianmag .com/travel/spice-trade-pepper-venice-180956856/#:~: text=And%20of%20all%20the%20spices,work%20for%20 an%20unskilled%20laborer.

Un po' di pepe. "Panforte di Siena." December 12, 2020. https://unpodipepe.ca/2020/12/12/panforte-di-siena/.

Veneto Inside. "The Regata of the Witches in Venice." January 6, 2012. https://www.venetoinside.com/events-in-veneto /event/the-regata-of-the-witches-in-venice/.

Venezia Tourism. "Regatta of Befana." Accessed October 6, 2022. https://www.venice-tourism.com/en/regatta-befana.

Venezia Tourism. "Witches Regatta." Accessed May 29, 2022. https://www.venezia-tourism.com/en/venice-events /witches-regatta.html.

Verein zum Schutz der Herkunftsbezeichnung Aachener Printen e. V. "Aachener Printen." Accessed March 10, 2022. https://www.aachenerprinten-gga.de/#features.

De Vieira Velho e Almeida, Celina. "The Christmas Consoada in Goa: Its Origin." December 18, 2019. https://www.herald goa.in/Goa/The-Christmas-Consoada-In-Goa-Its-Origin /154833.

Viswanadha, Mukund. "St. Maurice (d. 287)." Black Central Europe. Accessed January 27, 2023. https://blackcentral europe.com/biographies/st-maurice-mukund -viswanadha/.

Weiss-Krejci, Estella. "Allspice as Template for the Classic Maya K'an Sign." *The PARI Journal* Volume XII, No. 4, Spring 2012. https://www.yumpu.com/en/document /read/7475048/allspice-as-template-for-the-classic-maya -kan-sign-mesoweb.

Weiss-Krejci, Estella. "The Maya Corpse: Body Processing from Preclassic to Postclassic times in the Maya Highlands and Lowlands." ResearchGate. January 2006. https://www .researchgate.net/publication/273059464_The_Maya _corpse_Body_processing_from_Preclassic_to_Postclassic _times_in_the_Maya_highlands_and_lowlands.

Washington Crossing Historic Park. "Were the Hessians drunk when Washington attacked Trenton?" Accessed November 20, 2022. https://www.washingtoncrossingpark .org/hessians-drunk/#:~:text=We've%20all%20heard%20 the,myth%20rather%20than%20documented%20fact.

White, Joyce. "Virginia Corn Pone." A Taste of History with Joyce White. April 18, 2016. https://atasteofhistorywith joycewhite.blogspot.com/2016/04/corn-pone-in-literature -and-life.html?m=0.

Williams, Laura. "The long and sweet history of honey cake." The Jewish Star. September 9, 2020. https://www.thejewish star.com/stories/the-long-and-sweet-history-of-honey -cake, 19712.

Wingreen-Mason, Daria. "Cooking from the Collections: James Smithson's Gingerbread and more." Unbound Smith-sonian Libraries and Archives. December 16, 2011. https:// blog.library.si.edu/blog/2011/12/16/cooking-from-the -collections-james-smithsons-gingerbread-and-more /#YrRXyYPYrrd.

Y, Dr. "Edmond Albius, the Slave who launched the Vanilla Industry." November 14, 2013. https://afrolegends.com /2013/11/14/Edmond-albius-the-slave-who-launched-the -vanilla-industry/.

Założba Stiftung. "Sroka k ptačemu—Backen der 'sroka' zur Vogelhochzeit." January 22, 2021. https://www.youtube .com/watch?v=Ll3qNLrWD00&t=2s.

Index

To Write to the Author

If you wish to contact the author or would like more information about this book, please write to the author in care of Llewellyn Worldwide Ltd. and we will forward your request. Both the author and the publisher appreciate hearing from you and learning of your enjoyment of this book and how it has helped you. Llewellyn Worldwide Ltd. cannot guarantee that every letter written to the author can be answered, but all will be forwarded. Please write to:

Linda Raedisch
℅ Llewellyn Worldwide
2143 Wooddale Drive
Woodbury, MN 55125-2989
Please enclose a self-addressed stamped envelope for reply,
or $1.00 to cover costs. If outside the U.S.A., enclose
an international postal reply coupon.

Many of Llewellyn's authors have websites with additional information and resources. For more information, please visit our website at http://www.llewellyn.com.